Something really **NEW!**

NEW 1946 FORD SPORTSMAN'S CONVERTIBLE!

THERE'S A *Ford* IN YOUR FUTURE

1

FSB6611FR

Dedicated to the memory of
Dr. Thomas Garrett
The ultimate Sportsman enthusiast, expert,
and founder of the Seventy-One Society.

Printed and published in the United States of America

THE FORD SPORTSMAN

Including Mercury
1946-1948
By
Don Narus

www.newalbanybooks.com

Something really NEW!

NEW 1946 FORD SPORTSMAN'S CONVERTIBLE!

4

Contents

Smarter than
SMART!

THE FORD SPORTSMAN
INCLUDING MERCURY
1946-1948
BY DON NARUS

ISBN 978-1-4507-7620-2

Copyright 2011 Donald Narus

Published by
New Albany Books
2523 Pine Ridge Way S. B-1, Palm Harbor, Florida 34684

First Edition
0123456789

Narus, Donald J. (Don)
  1. Ford History, 2. Ford Sportsman, 3. Ford Woodies, 4. Mercury Sportsman,
    5. Ford Convertibles, 6. Mercury Convertibles 7. Woodie Convertibles

www.newalbanybooks.com

Something really NEW!

BIG NEW 100 H. P. V-8

makes Ford the liveliest performer of all the low-priced cars! New die-ring aluminum pistons and new balanced carburetion make the big Ford V-8 thrifty on gas and oil!

IT TAKES A TRUNK

There's room galore in this new luggage compartment . . . just as there's room galore for six grown-ups in the wide leather seats!

NEW 1946 FORD SPORTSMAN'S CONVERTIBLE!

Outside and inside there never was a car like this before! The new Ford Sportsman's Convertible is really two cars in one! Ford designers have combined the paneled smartness of the station wagon and the touch-a-button convenience of the convertible!

JUST TOUCH A BUTTON

. . . and in 30 seconds you have a snug "sedan" that's weather-tight! With the top up or with it down, the Sportsman's Convertible is a beauty for looks!

NEW OVERSIZED BRAKES

. . . self-centering and hydraulic . . . with big 12-inch brake drums . . . to give you smooth, straight-line stops on all road surfaces. Quiet? Easy-acting. Long-life linings!

THERE'S A *Ford* **IN YOUR FUTURE**

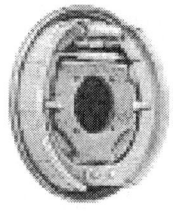

You're out Front in a Ford!

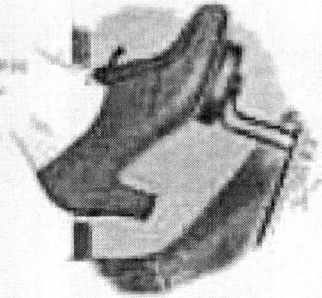

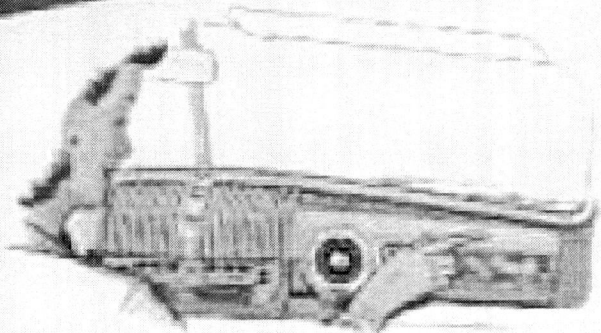

There's a Ford in your future

Credits and Acknowledgments

Thank you Ford Motor Company Archives and Chrysler Corporation for information and factory photographs. To Bill Large, thanks for your willingness to share your story and photos, priceless. To Gerald Greenfield for sharing your material and photos. To Terry Johnson, a big thanks, John Mesloh, Hyman Ltd. Classic Cars, Henry Miller, Alyn Edwards, Gene Hetland, Mike DeViriendt,Dennis Smith, Tim Burton. Information was also obtained from the Seventy-One Society Newsletters, V-8 Times, Richard Adams Sr.,Hemmings Motor News/David Gooly. Some of the photos used were obtained from various sources and were identified where-ever possible, if your name was left out, I apologize, it was either not readily available or unintentional. Also a big thank you to the contributors of Flickr.com, Yahoo.com images, Google.com, the RM Auctions/The Nick Alexander Collection and conceptcarz.com.

A Special Thanks to Dave Kuffel whose help through out this whole project was invaluable. Your material and input were indispensable. I appreciate your participation and contribution.

Front and Rear Cover photo by: Dave Kuffel

FORD'S OUT FRONT IN TOWN... AND COUNTRY!

The new Ford convertible is right at home in the smartest settings! And its dashing style is combined with touch-a-button convenience ... in just thirty seconds this open car becomes a snug "sedan"! All kinds of room for six people ... all kinds of "go" with that lively 100-horsepower Ford V-8 engine.

The new Ford station wagon carries 8 in luxury! Seats can be easily removed for light hauling. The husky body is fashioned of rugged maple, with beautiful birch or gumwood panels. The big seat cushions are covered in smart, long-wearing Vinyl plastic leather. In station wagon style, Ford's the leader. Ford has built more station wagons than all other car manufacturers combined.

Plenty of room for luggage in the rear compartment — even when the removable seats are in place!

LISTEN ... The FORD-Bob Crosby Show—CBS, Wednesdays, 9:30-10 p.m., E.D.T. ... The FORD Sunday Evening Hour—ABC Sundays, 8-9 p.m., E.D.T.

There's a Ford in your future

Note: The play on words must have irritated Chrysler

12

Introduction

It all began in 1945, when Henry Ford II commissioned Ford designer E.T. (Bob) Gergorie to build some kind of Beach Buggy, that could be used at the Ford Southampton, NY summer home. Gergorie came up with a "Woodie" convertible based on a unused Model "A" chassis that he found up at the Ford Iron Mountain, Michigan facility. He named it an "Estate Wagon".

The Model "A" Estate Wagon* was built on a 1931 chassis, it had a basic Model "A" front clip with a 1930 radiator surround, it also had 1930 pedals, steering column and mechanical brakes. The shocks were from a 1932, instruments were from 1938 and 1939, the steering wheel was 1940. the solid wheels are also 1940. Headlights were sealed beams, the bumpers are modified 1941 Super Deluxe. The dash, windshield frame and convertible top are custom made. A lot of the wood body hardware is borrowed from a regular station wagon. The car was maroon with matching leather upholstery. The door curtains are ridged while the tailgate window is flexible and flips inside for storage. It was a neat one-of-a-kind car. Henry II loved it. So much so that he instructed Gregoire to consider doing one on a 1946 chassis.

As the war drew to a close the word in the industry was that Chrysler was planning a whole line of wood bodied cars for 1946 based on their successful pre-war Town & Country. Henry II went to Gregorie with thoughts of jazzing up their 1946 cars. A whole new body design was out of the question if they were to get production rolling as soon as possible, only a face lifted 1942 could accomplish a quick re-entry into the post war market. But a wood body convertible might be just the ticket. Gregorie and his top illustrator, Ross Cousins, made some sketches, Henry II liked them and work got underway to build a prototype.

The design team took their drawings and with engineers re-worked a regular steel bodied convertible at Iron Mountain. Removing the metal skin of the convertible they were left with a steel skeleton to which they attached a wood skin. For the most part things worked out well, but there were some glitches. The stock convertible wrap around rear fenders did not work. The problem was solved by using sedan delivery rear fenders, but then the stock 1946 tail lights did not work and that problem was solved by using stock 1941 tail lights. The seats were upholstered with leather faces and leatherette trim. Power window lifts from the Lincoln were used for the door and quarter windows. Front door vents were crank out, not push out. These were luxury items not usually found as standard equipment in a low price car. The finished product was very attractive, and sporty. They called it the "Sportsman" and it would be available as a Ford and Mercury.

That first prototype was built in October 1945 and put on display in Dearborn. Three months later, in December another prototype was built. To garner as much publicity as possible the initial prototype was delivered and presented to movie actress Ella Raines on December 25, 1945; beating the Chrysler Town and Country convertible debut by two months.

Plagued by material shortages and strikes, full production of the Sportsman did not get underway until July 1946. Both Ford and Mercury shared the same body; the metal skeleton built by Murray Corporation** with wood applied at the Iron Mountain, Michigan facility along side station wagon bodies. The finished bodies were then shipped to various assembly plants around the country.

During the entire production period from the first month to the last there were continual changes to the wood body, some were subtle, some were obvious, so much so that no two bodies are alike. Basically the tweaking resulted in three wood body patterns, simply labeled: "A", "B", and "C". What created the differences was how the vertical and horizontal pieces were used. What permitted these changes was the metal skeleton to which they were attached. Unlike the Chrysler Town & Country, or the Ford Station Wagon for that matter, the Sportsman wood skin was not structural. It was thinner, therefore easier to make minor or major changes.

Ford and Chrysler were the only two major auto manufactures to build wood bodied cars in house. Chrysler had their Pekin Wood Plant and Ford had Iron Mountain. Ultimately the Ford and Mercury Sportsman did not fare well in sales and were discontinued, Mercury after one model year Ford after three. Although Ford went on to be the leader in station wagon sales, and become the indisputable "Wagon Master".

*The Model "A" Estate Wagon although built in 1945 was registered as a 1941. This was due to War Department regulations, that no civilian cars were to be built during the war. The Estate Wagon was eventually given to Bob Gergorie,, and he used it at his Florida home for some years before it was then sold to a collector.
**Murray supplied the skeleton according to their History Bio. They had been supplying sheet metal parts to Ford since the 1920s.

In 1945 Henry Ford II commissioned in-house designer E.T. "Bob" Gregorie to fashion a beach buggy for his Southampton,NY summer home. Gregorie came up with what amounts to a Model "A" Sportsman. Henry II loved the car and ordered one to be built on a 1946 chassis.

(Left), the "Estate Wagon" ready for delivery. (Right), Bob Gregorie and company worked up a post World War II Sportsman design, one of the drawings by Ross Cousins shows an updated Estate Wagon. The idea looked feasible based on the conventional convertible. They got the green light to pursue the design, and the rest, as they say, is history.

Photos from Ford Motor Company Archives

The first Ford Sportsman prototype, built in October of 1945, was extensively photographed at the factory. It was then presented to movie actress Ella Raines on December 25, 1945. <u>Note:</u> the absence of the "Sportsman" script on the hood and deck lid also no rear fender splash guards. The color of this car was maroon.

Photos from Ford Motor Company Archives

The stock convertible fender would not work because of the wrap around, to solve the problem the rear fender from the 1946 sedan delivery was used. The same held true for the stock tail lights. They did not work either, so stock 1941 tail lights were used.

Early deck lids had the center cross bar set high, which created a water dam. This was corrected by lowering the cross bar and beveling the top edge. With this change the vertical center bar which was one continuous piece, was now two pieces. Iron Mountain engineers stated that reason for this change was to improve strength.

The upper rear panel on early cars **(left)** was a tight butt fit to the quarter panel, which did not allow for expansion or contraction of the wood. Later versions were cut slightly shorter, a chrome filler strip **(right)** was inserted to cover the gap and prevent leaks.

Photos from Ford Motor Company and various sources

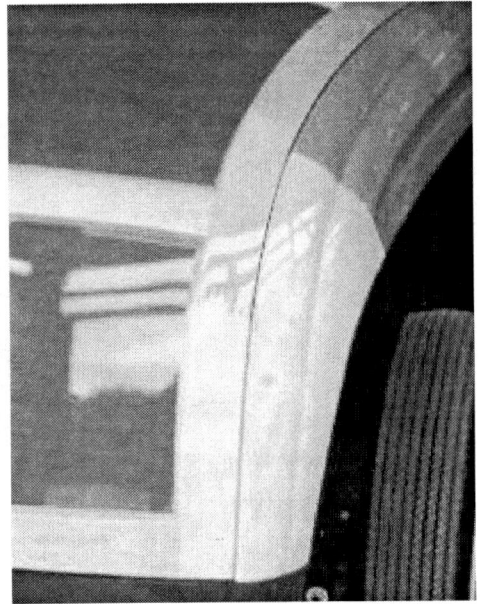

Some of the continuous changes included the use of finger joints. The lower part of the rear quarter in the early prototype was pieced together with a finger joint (**left**), later it was changed to a lap joint **(center and right),** an economy move. It was cheaper to make the lap joint. The outer deck lid frame was made up of three pieces on each side, in the early cars the lower piece was longer, on the later cars it was shorter. The outside frame work on the early models was narrower, quarter inch wider on the later.

Deck lid hinges used on the Sportsman **(left)** were low profile and much smaller then those used on the Chrysler Town & Country, **(right)** which were massive and looked like boat cleats. One of the reason Ford could use the smaller hinge was weight. The Ford deck lid was lighter compared to the Chrysler. Ford used collapsible arms for lid support, like the one used to support the hood, while Chrysler used two spring loaded tubes, one a each side to support the heavier lid. Both Ford and Chrysler used hard wood for framing; Ford used Maple and Birch, Chrysler used White Ash.

Photos from Ford Motor Company Archives, Dave Kuffel, authors Collection and yahoo.com pics

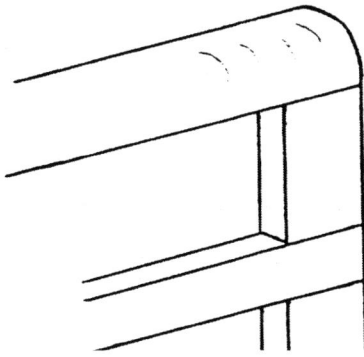

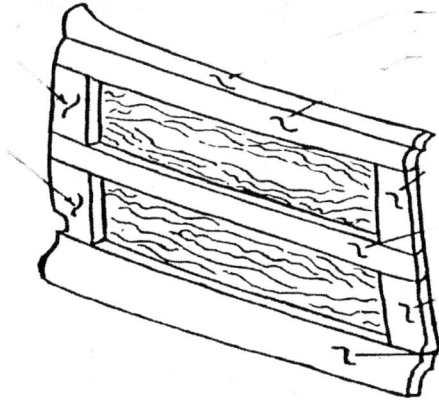

The "A" pattern used on all 1946 Ford and Mercury Sportsman
Bodies number 1- 1,114 (except 918 & 1107) total built 1,112

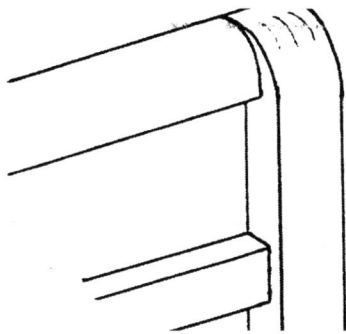

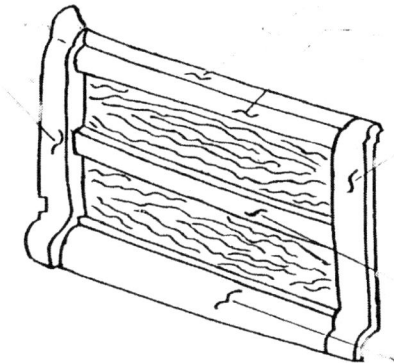

The "B" pattern used on most 1947 Ford Sportsman
Bodies number 1,115 – 2,994, total built 1,182

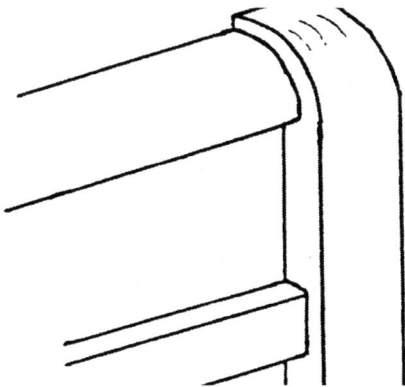

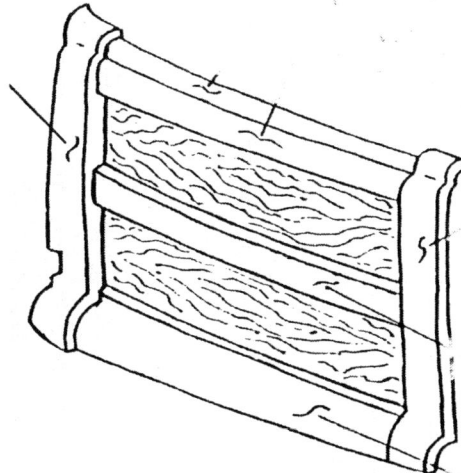

The "C" pattern used on part of the 1947 and all 1948 Ford Sportsman
Bodies number 2,995-3,725 total built 731

Drawings and stats from the Seventy-One Society Newsletter

The "A" pattern on **(left)**, used on all 1946 Ford and Mercury Sportsman through December 1946. The "B" pattern on **(right)**, used on '47s through most of July 1947.

The "C" pattern used on 1947 and all 1948s from July through November 1947; it had the shortest run. This pattern is found on most surviving Sportsman today.

Photos from Gerald Greenfield, Nick Alexander Collection and Macatawa Bay Boat Works

The Chrysler Town and Country body was all structural wood, mounted on a floor pan.

The Ford Sportsman door **(left)** was structurally steel, whereas the Chrysler door **(right)** was structurally wood with a metal plate mounted to the inside to which the window regulator and door lock mechanism were mounted. A leading edge steel plate was used for the hinges. The T&C door was prone to sagging. The Ford station wagon and Sportsman shared the same exterior door handle. **(right photo).**

The Chrysler upper back panel **(left),** was a heavy solid piece with a step/ tenon joint, a spacer was not necessary. The Ford upper back panel **(right)** was thinner and fastened to the metal skeleton. A spacer was necessary for expansion and contraction.

Photos from Ford Motor Company, Chrysler Corporation, Ed Wong Collection, Matawac Bay Boat Works and Don Narus

The first Ford Sportsman prototype was built in October 1945.

The first Mercury Sportsman prototype was built in April 1946.

Photos from Ford Motor Company Archives

Chapter One
1946

Ford and Mercury Sportsman full production did not get underway until July 1946. A prototype was built in October 1945, followed by another in December 1945. With the exception of the prototypes the Sportsman metal skeleton production bodies were supplied by Murray Corporation of Detroit.*

On December 25th 1945 Ford presented the first Sportsman to movie actress Ella Raines and by doing so beat out the Chrysler Town and Country Convertible debut by two months.

Ford would compete with Chrysler with two models, the Ford and Mercury. The Mercury being an upgrade. Both cars were priced below Chrysler. The Ford at $1,982. and Mercury at $2,209. A total of 723 Ford Sportsman and 205 Mercury Sportsman were produced for the model year 1946. Chrysler produced 1,935 Town & Country convertibles for 1946 priced at $2,725.

Production of the 1946 Ford and Mercury Sportsman was not without its problems. Fit for one thing. Initially there were fit problems, doors and deck lids, then there was a design flaw, the deck lid cross member was placed to high and created a water dam. This coupled with strikes and material shortages slowed production and effected the overall numbers. Once the strikes were settled and the problems resolved production continued at a reasonable pace in keeping with demand.

The one casualty for 1946 was the Mercury Sportsman. With little to no advertising, and a higher price tag, ($227. over Ford), the public response to the Mercury Sportsman was cool. After a short run (July to September 1946) only 205 units were built. In a September 7, 1946 press release, Lincoln-Mercury Division announced that there would be no 1947 model.

In comparison to the Chrysler Town & Country the Sportsman offered luxury items as standard, (full leather interior and power windows) not found in the higher priced T&C. Just as attractive as the T&C and priced $743. less, it was a good buy, but expensive for the Ford buyer.

*Murray Corporation had been supplying Ford with sheet metal and body components since the 1920s (source:History of Murray Corp.).

In order to garner publicity and establish a Hollywood connection, the first Ford Sportsman was presented to movie actress Ella Raines on December 25, 1945. It was photographed extensively.

Photos from Ford Motor Company Archives

The first built Mercury Sportsman was publicly introduced sitting atop a Lincoln-Mercury float during the Golden Jubilee parade in Detroit, Michigan on June 1, 1946. This was the only publicity the Mercury received. No ads, no brochure, no press kit.

Photos from the Bill Large collection

The Ford and Mercury Sportsman interior was available in Tan, Red and Gray leather. (The seat faces were leather) trimmed with matching leatherette. Luxury for its day.

Standard interiors for Ford and Mercury steel bodied convertibles were a combination of leather bolsters and Bedford Cord cloth, trimmed with leatherette. Door panels were the same for the woodie Sportsman and the steel convertibles, trimmed in leatherette.

Photos from Daniel Schmitt and Co. and RM Auctions

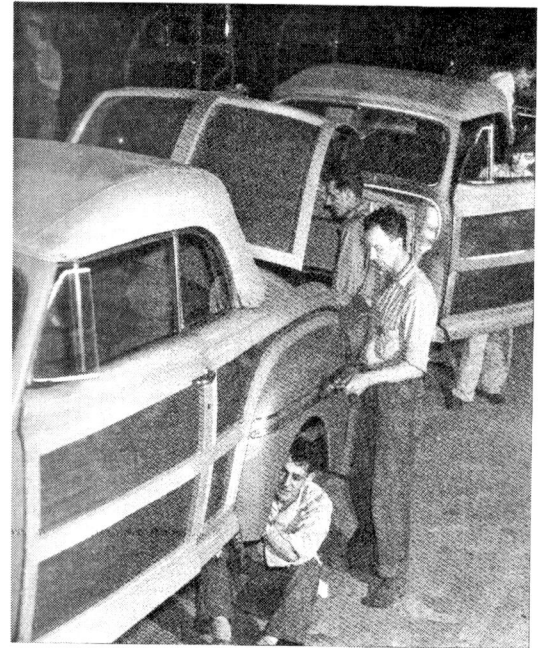

Sportsman assembly line at Iron Mountain, hardware and trim are being installed. Ford and Mercury bodies were assembled on the same line, along side station wagons.

Iron Mountain Michigan assembly, **(left),** the hydraulic window system borrowed from Lincoln, was installed prior to the wood body application. **(right),** cowl weather strip is installed as a final step in the assembly process. All hand labor. No robots in 1946.

Photos from Ford Motor Company Archives and Dave Kuffle collection

In 1949 **(left)** Chrysler adopted the Ford skeleton **(right)** method of construction.

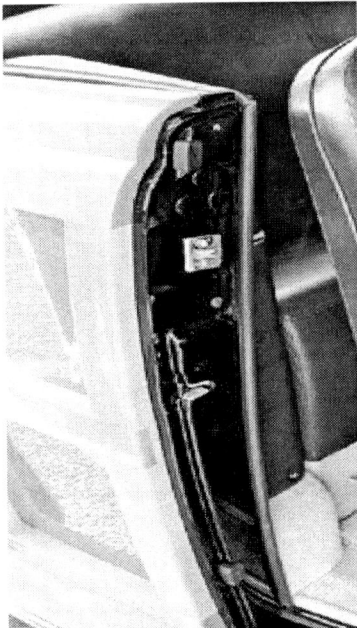

__1946-48 Ford quarter__   __1949 Chrysler quarter__   __1946-48 Ford door__ __1949 Chrysler door__

There are obvious similarities to Ford, in the way the 1949 Town & Country was built.

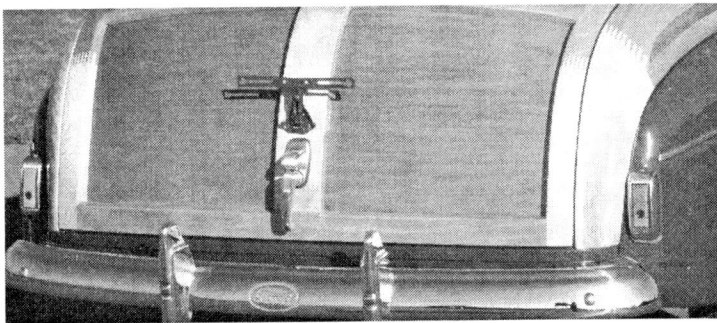

The '46 Ford deck lid horizontal members were much narrower than the '46 Chrysler.
Ford mounted the taillights on the fenders, Chrysler mounted them on the wood frame.
Ford had a integrated tail/stop light, Chrysler used a single center mounted stop light.

Photos from Ford Motor Archives, Chrysler Corporation, RM Auctions, Macatawa Boat Works and Tim Burton Collection

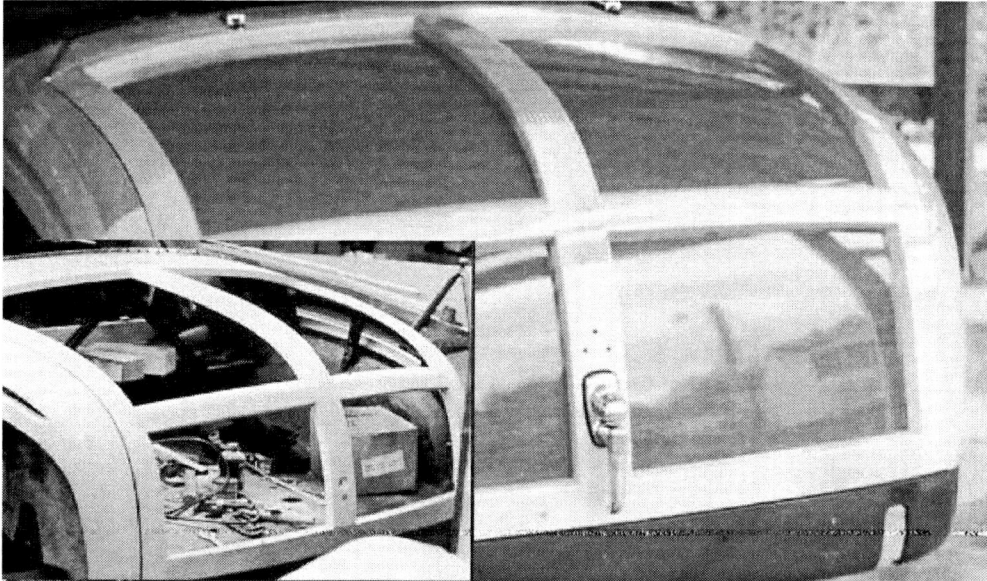

The Ford insert plywood panel was one piece. Which added to the rigidity of the deck lid. Repairs were costly. If damage occurred it usually required replacement of the entire panel.

The Chrysler deck lid was substantial and much heavier than the Sportsman. (**Note: the thickness of the wood in the inset photos.**) Unlike Ford, Chrysler construction was always consistent. Horizontal pieces were always one piece, vertical members were made from two pieces using finger joints. Ford used a one piece insert plywood panel, while Chrysler used four separate veneer covered metal panels. The only consistency in Ford's construction was the one piece plywood deck lid insert panel.

Photos from Macawata Bay Boat Works and H.A.M.B.

29

A word about the deck lid

All the Mahogany Veneer plywood inner panels are flat except for the deck lid. The deck lid looks like it has four separate panels but instead it is a large single panel. The panel is made up of several layers, each layer is glued up and formed under pressure over a full-size wood form, which provides the compound curves. The outer Mahogany Veneer layer is glued on in three separate pieces. This prevents cracking of the veneer under pressure. The single panel gives the deck lid its strength. It is the only only part of the Sportsman that is structurally wood. The inner steel frame work is used only to hold the inner liner in place and provides an attachment place for the support arms. The Maple frame work is merely attached to the panel. The deck lid is strong and light weight but expensive to replace.

(left), the panel is formed in a mold under pressure.**(right)**, panel ready for sanding.

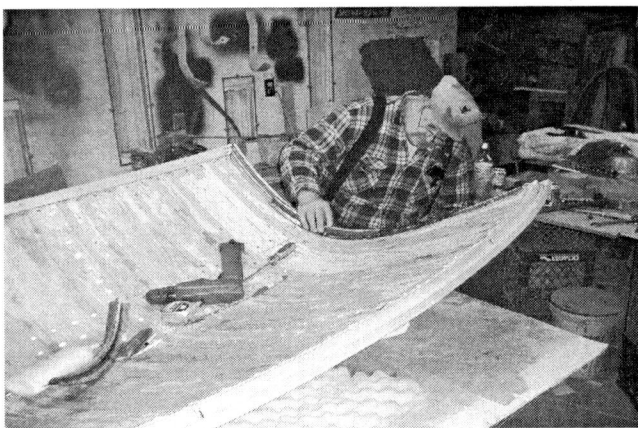

(Left), metal frame work is attached to inner panel. **(Right)**, finished panel varnished.

Photos from Bill Large Collection

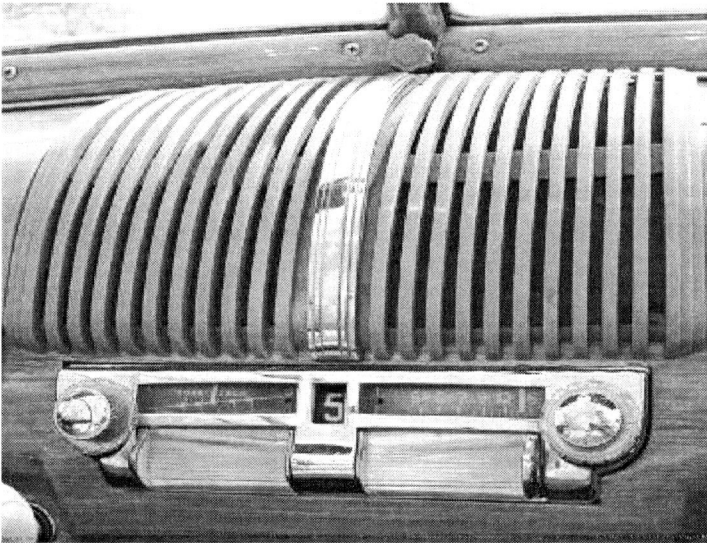

The Ford radio grille dominated the dashboard. The wonder-bar radio was the popular choice of Sportsman buyers. The optional electric clock mirrored the speedometer.

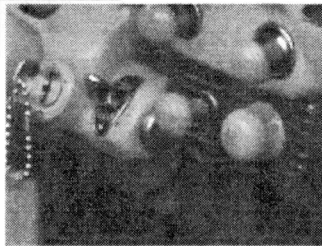

Under left side of dash plastic starter button. Ignition switch and column lock. The driver had control of all four power windows. The power windows came from Lincoln.

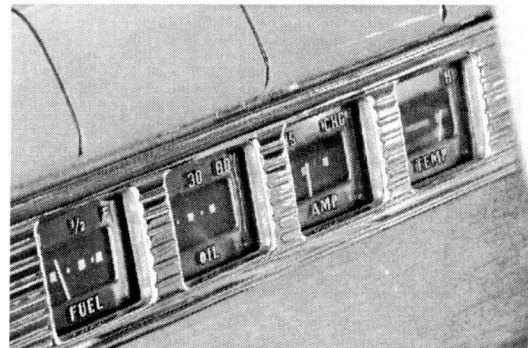

The glove box door chrome trim with logo balanced the opposite side gauge bezel.

Photos from David Kuffel and Daniel Schmitt and Company

In 2009 a number of cars from Ford collector Nick Alexander were put up for auction. Including five Ford Sportsman and one rare Mercury Sportsman. The results of the auction set the market price for both models at that time. In 1973 noted auto historian Robert Gottleib predicted that within ten years the Sportsman would be worth over $10,000. He was right, and in 2009 that prediction grew twenty times plus.

A late 1946 built after January 1946, with "B" pattern wood body, chassis No. 799A1236365 Dark Slate Gray Metallic code M-3991, part of the Nick Alexander collection was sold at the RM Monterey auction in 2009 , for $242,000.

A 1946, 99A1307387, on the block at the Gooding & Company auction, Amelia Isl, FL.

Photos from Nick Alexander Collection/RM Auctions and Gooding & Company Auctions

Basically the steering wheel and dashboard are the same for all years. Standard equipment for the Sportsman included, a wind-up clock, (elec.optional) full leather seating and power windows, which were borrowed from the Lincoln. Such standard luxury features were not to be found in the more pricey Chrysler Town and Country.

Chrysler's Town & Country luxury appointments included color keyed plastic trim, electric clock, lavish use of chrome, comfort-master flow through heating/ventilating system, Fluid-Drive transmission and dual spotlights. Standard upholstery: leather and Bedford Cord cloth, full leather optional. Note: leather door check straps, 1946 only.

Photos from Nick Alexander collection/RM Auctions and Tim Burton Collection

Original '46

Terry Johnson is a very discerning car collector, so when the opportunity came up to acquire an original 1946 Ford Sportsman he did not hesitate. It would become the companion piece to his original 1947 Chrysler Town and Country convertible Terry took possession of 99A-1063779 a Navy Blue, paint code M-3982 Sportsman in the summer of 2010. The car essentially is all original, body number is 239 in the "A" pattern, with original wood except for the deck lid. The interior is all original except for the front seating area. The top is new and the paint has been refreshed. The car was built in August 1946 and delivered new by Northwestern Motor Car Co. in Milwaukee, Wisconsin, on September 24, 1946 to Theodore Matt. Full price $2,053.93 Since owning the car the only repairs Terry has made is to the radio. It now works, as does everything else. According to Terry, *"the car drives like a dream"*.

The 1946 Ford Sportsman is displayed with Terry's original 1947 T&C convertible, The accessories shown: the side view mirrors, bumper wings, grille guard and wheel trim rings are all original to the period and were dealer installed after delivery.

Photos provided by owner Terry Johnson

Body 239 is obviously an early "A" pattern wood body, note the absence of chrome spacers on the upper back panel. (**see inset photo at top**). The deck lid was replaced with the newer lower center crossbar. The earlier higher crossbar caused a water dam and eventually rotted the deck lid. A common problem with the old style lid.

The top was replaced. According to the original bill of sale the car was delivered new

on September 24, 1946 with a out-the-door price of $2,053.93 The interior is all original except for the front seating area. Floor mat and door panels are still in good shape. Everything works, surprisingly the power windows are still in working order.

Photos provided by owner Terry Johnson

Ford used spring loaded bent arms (same as hood support) for the deck lid support. Trunk walls and lid were lined with fiber covered cardboard and a rubber floor mat.

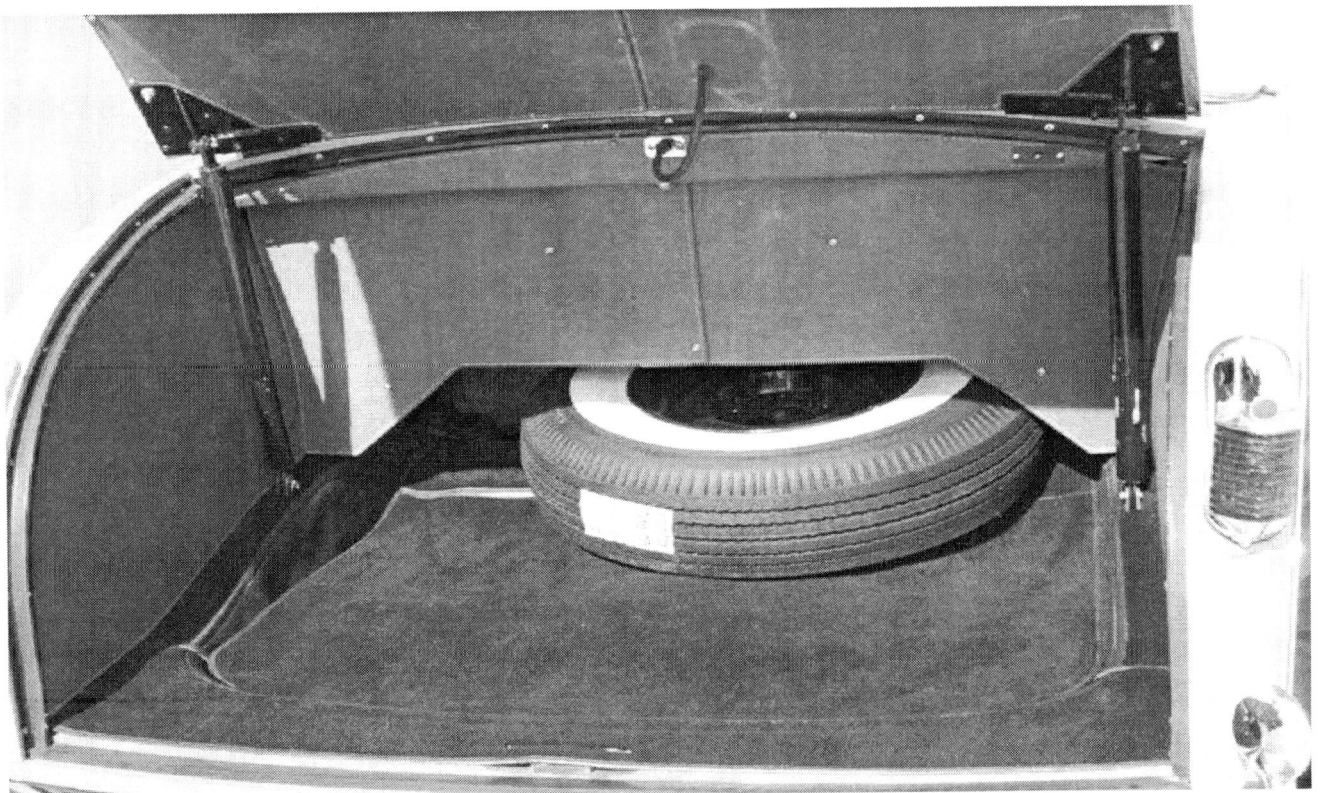

Chrysler used spring loaded tubes as deck lid supports. Trunk walls and inside lid were lined with leatherette covered cardboard and a carpeted floor mat.

Photos from Google search

From Scratch

Building a Sportsman like the factory is not an easy task. Early in the process the Sportsman went from idea, to drawing, to prototype. The idea was to take a steel body convertible, strip off the metal skin and replace it with a wood skin. Sounds easy, but is it?

There were several things to consider. First there was the trunk. The idea was to square off the trunk. Make it twelve inches wider, which required the rear quarters to be re-worked. Just stripping the metal skin off just did not work. So a new skeletal frame had to be built. Remember,during actual production they were not going to take steel convertibles off the line strip them and build a sportsman. From the "B" post back a new skeletal frame had to be fabricated. Second a new inner fender, trunk floor and splash pan had to be made. Once the prototype was built drawings could be made. The job of building the skeletal body for production was then farmed out to Murray Corp.

So who in the world would take on the task of duplicating that first prototype? The Browns, father and son team, of The Sportsman Restoration shop did. Taking a stock steel convertible they proceeded to build a Sportsman body *"from scratch"*. It took them four years to complete. When done it established the Browns once and for all, as the undisputed premier Sportsman body builders. If you want a Sportsman and can't find one, no problem you can always have the "The Sportsman Restoration Shop", build one for you *"From Scratch"*.

Take a sold conventional 1946 Ford convertible body, strip off the metal skin, fabricate a steel skeleton frame and just like Ford you have a prototype Sportsman body.

Photos by Brown and Son dba The Sportsman Shop

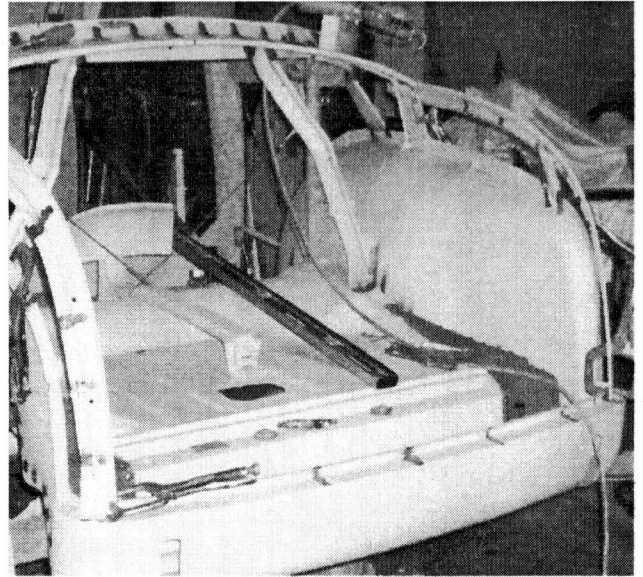

(left),the original trunk had to be re-worked,**(right),**a new floor and wheel wells made.

(left),rear wheel wells were fabricated by hand.**(right),** the collar that would surround the rear seat was fabricated off the car and was a critical of the overall skeleton body.

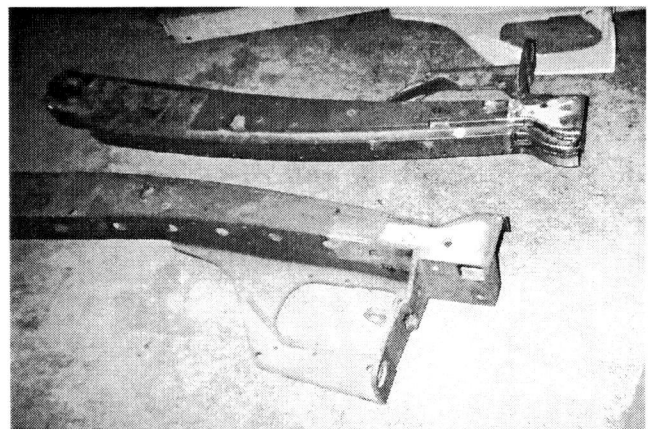

(left),collar,upper back panel brace and wheel wells are welled in place**(right),**"B"posts are removed, refurbished and re-installed. The rest of the skeleton install will follow.

Photos by Brown and Son dba The Sportsman Shop

38

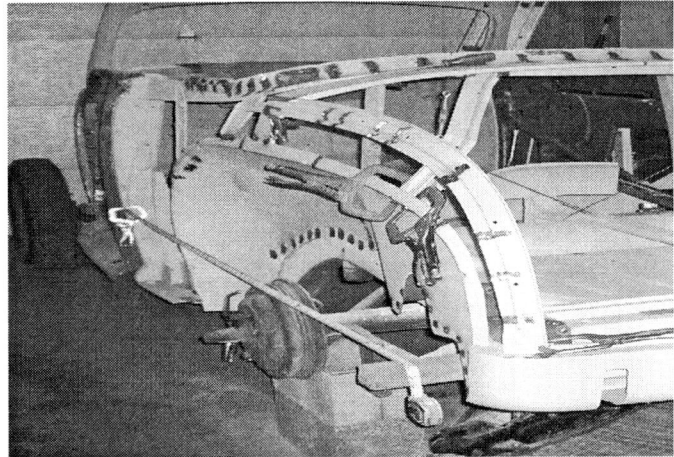

In comparison **(original Ford body on left, Brown's body on right)** the two skeletal bodies are identical in every way. Once finished off there would no way of telling them apart. It's a tribute to the patience and craftsmanship of the father and son team.

The finished body is an exact copy of an early "A" pattern. Made perfectly. Like Ford did it in 1945, right down to the lap joint of the upper back panel **(check inset photo)**.

Photos by Brown and Son dba The Sportsman Restoration Shop

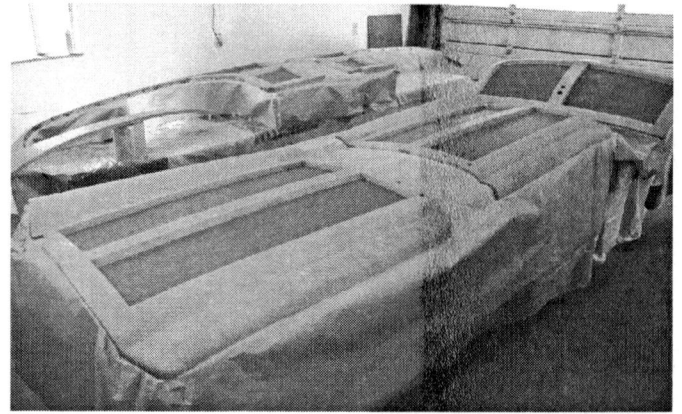

The preferred way to restore a Sportsman is to remove the wood skin, refinish it off the car and re-install. The metal skeleton is treated and painted with the wood removed. The above and below photos will give you some idea of how thin the wood panels are.

The finished car is in Black paint code M-1724 shows off the wood nicely. Maple framing over Mahogany plywood panels in the "A" pattern. All 1946 models used the same wood pattern.

Photos from Alternative Automotive Design

Sportsman Fever

Dennis Smith caught Sportsman fever in 1999, while he and his son Daryl were attending the "Great American Woody Show" in Los Angeles. Which was held on the grounds of the Petersen Automotive Museum, on display during show week was a beautiful 1946 Sportsman. It was love at first sight. Dennis began his search for one of his own almost immediately. Actually the job of finding a Sportsman fell to his son. Daryl spent the better part of year contacting every known Sportsman owner, without any luck. Then came an Email from Art Bjornestad, who was willing to sell his 1946 Sportsman. A deal was quickly struck. Ironically it was the very same Sportsman they viewed at the Petersen Museum. The 1946 Pheasant Red 99A1237320, body number 763, was once owned by Dr. Tom Garrett. It was completely restored in the early 1990s. It has won many awards with the most coveted being the one won at "Wave Crest" in 2006. The Sportsman is a family affair, with wife Darlene keeping the car clean and son Daryl doing all the mechanical maintenance.

Photos from owners Dennis and Darlene Smith

A Word About Advertising

Ford launched its Sportsman advertising campaign with a two page full color ad in the March 5, 1946 issue of the Saturday Evening Post. Four months ahead of actual production. Fords tag line was "Something Really New" coupled with its overall slogan, "There's a Ford in your Future". It was followed up with full color single page ads continuing with the same tag line. This was followed with a two color (red and black) single page ad and a new tag line "Ford's Out Front", which was followed by a shared full color single page ad with another tag line "You're Out Front In a Ford". An interesting observation of the car illustrated in these ads. It showed a full length belt line stainless molding, and white walls that were two sided, such as those used in the 1930s

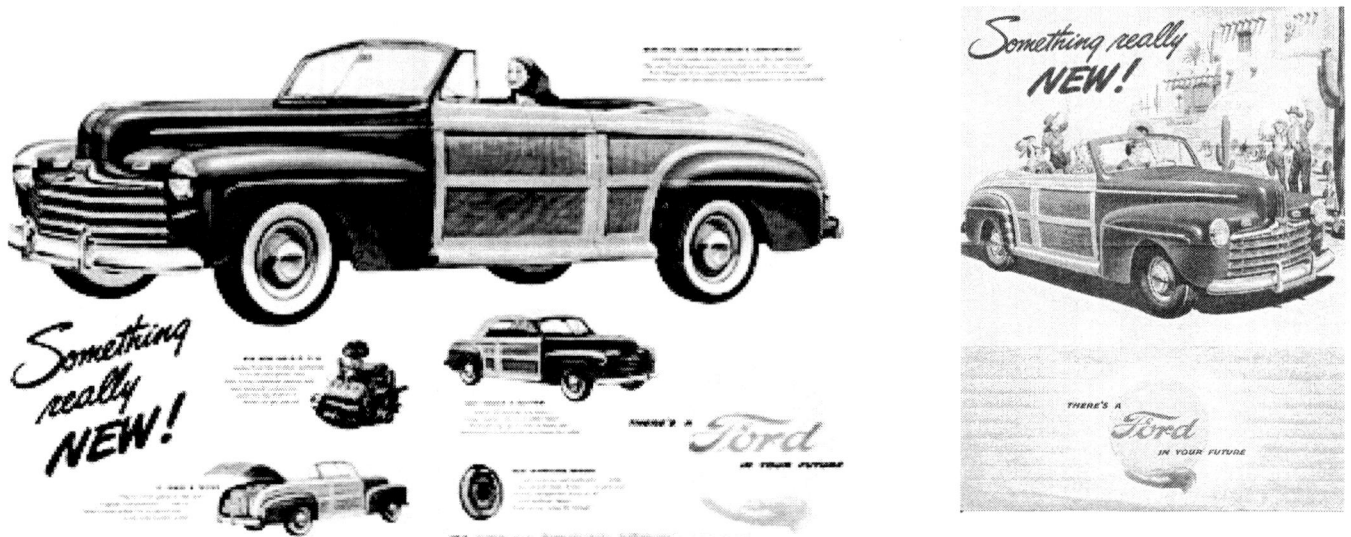

The ad campaign highlighted the 100hp V-8, larger brakes and a roomy trunk

The single page full color ad and single page two color ad were similar with different tag lines. A black and white single page ad also appeared south of the border. The last ad **(right)** was a shared ad with a partial Sportsman and appeared in September 1946.

Ads are from the authors collection

The New Ford Sportsman

In addition to the ads Ford issued a full color fold-out brochure, continuing the smart theme, "Smarter Than Smart". Emphasizing the 100hp V-8 , power top and large trunk capacity. Curiously, the Sportsman illustration in the sales brochure showed the car with black wall tires, while all but one magazine ad showed the car with whitewalls. The brochure was issued early in 1946.

From the authors collection

1946   1896

50 YEARS OF PROGRESS

Ford

OUT FRONT THEN — OUT FRONT NOW

Something Really New

There's a *Ford* in your future!

1946 FORD *Sportsman's* CONVERTIBLE

SETS THE PACE IN POSTWAR STYLE AND VALUE !

Upper photo, dealer showroom poster. **Lower photo,** dealer promo postcard.

Photos from Dave Kuffel

The first Mercury Sportsman was built in April 1946 and introduced to the public on June 1, 1946. There was no advertising, no brochure. Production started in July 1946. It did not sell well. In September 1946 Mercury Division discontinued production.

Photos from Ford Motor Company archives

Mercury 1946

The Mercury Sportsman is somewhat of a conundrum, invoking more questions than answers. Why a Mercury Sportsman in the first place? It was never advertised, there were no brochures. Introduction to the public came in a parade, atop the Lincoln-Mercury Float, sharing the stage with a 1946 Lincoln.
Its run was short lived. The first example was made in April 1946. It was photographed extensively by the factory, and first shown to the public in Detroit's Golden Jubilee Parade on June 1, 1946. It went into production in July 1946 and on September 7, 1946 the Mercury Division announced that there would be no 1947 model. The reason for the discontinuation was never given, although it was surmised that poor sales was the leading factor. A total of 205 were built. Then there was the price factor, the Mercury was priced $227. higher than the Ford version.

In a 1973 issue of the Seventy-One Society newsletter, Sportsman guru, Tom Garrett had considered the Mercury Sportsman and wrote: "In retrospect, considering the higher price of Mercury's, it would have seemed more logical to make the Sportsman exclusively Mercury, as this line was more expensive to begin with. But far be it from me to try and analyze the motives of Ford Motor Company."

In my opinion neither Ford or Mercury models were meant to be volume cars. Where wood body cars were concerned Ford concentrated their efforts in building station wagons. The Sportsman was a traffic builder. Put in a showroom to draw attention. Not a great deal of money was spent on advertising Unlike Chrysler which had a series of magazine ads in 1946 and 1947, and a five page full color brochure displaying a full line of wood bodied cars. Ford had three magazine ads and a two page folder for 1946 only.

Price comparison: For 1946 the Ford Sportsman was priced at $1,982. and the Mercury at $2,209. as compared to the Chrysler Town & Country convertible which was priced at $2,725. Given the price difference of $516. between the Mercury and Chrysler and given Mercury's market position, it probably would have competed a lot better with Chrysler. Irony has a funny way of playing out. Chrysler was priced higher and was more prestigious in 1946, but in today's collector car market, the Sportsman commands higher dollars.

All the factory photos of the Mercury Sportsman are of the prototype car produced in April 1946. It was painted Silver Sand, paint code M3992. Ford's Iron Mountain Plant Manager, Walter Nelson, owned the first Mercury Sportsman.

Photos from Ford Motor Company Archives

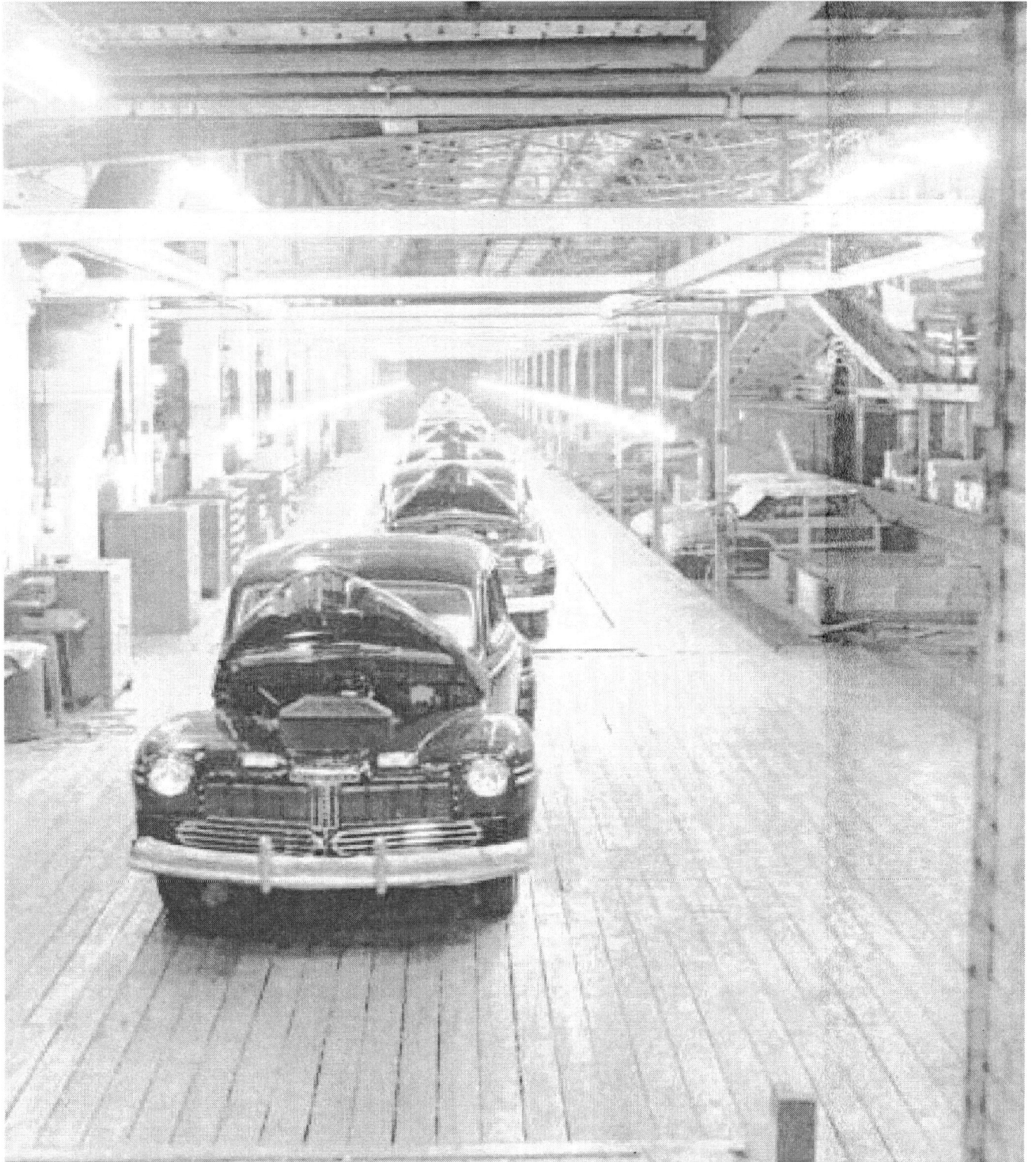

Mercury final assembly. The photo is dated April 1946. <u>Note:</u> Check the right side of the photo there appears to be two Sportsman bodies waiting for insertion into the assembly process. One of those bodies would be the first Mercury Sportsman.

Photo from the Ford Motor Company Archives

The Mercury (**left**) differed from Ford (**right**) in dash trim and shade of wood-grain.

Both Mercury and Ford used Red high lights and similar wheel trim rings.

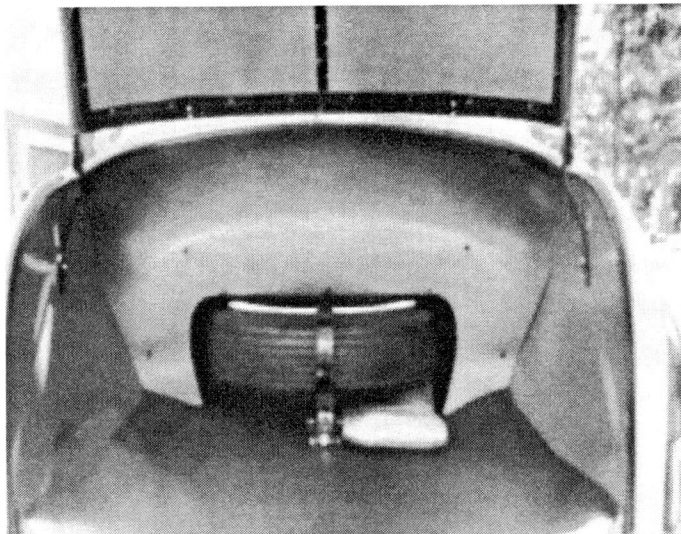

Mercury (**left**) and Ford (**right**) trunks were identical. The configuration was the same, both used coated cardboard liners with a rubber mat, simple, neat and clean.

Photos from Bill Large and Yahoo.com images,

The Mercury grille took its styling cue from the Lincoln. Lots of die cast chrome.

Mercury and Ford front fenders were similar but not interchangeable. The Mercury sported more bright metal trim, from die cast fender top spears to stainless molding

Except for stainless molding trim pieces; Mercury and Ford rear fender were identical.
Photos from Bill Large, RM Auctions and yahoo.com images

Building a Mercury Sportsman

It took Bill Large over six years to finish building his immaculate 1946 Mercury Sportsman in Greenfield Green paint code M-3990. Body number is 146, initially built in July 1946. No detail was overlooked. Being authentic was his goal. "*Build it like Ford would have, maybe even better.*" In 2008 he entered his car in the Meadow Brook Concourse; won the "*Traditional Beauty Award*". Patience and perfection is all it took.

Photos from owner Bill Large

51

In 2002 Bill Large had finished building a new home and workshop. Retired, he was ready for a project. He had been researching the Mercury Sportsman for some time and decided that this was the car he wanted. Small problem, there weren't any around. The Mercury Sportsman is a rather rare car, only 205 were produced in 1946. If Bill was going to have his Sportsman, he was going to have to build one.

In March of 2002 Bill answered an ad in Hemmings for a basket case 1946 Ford Sportsman Body; perfect. Coincidentally the body was located at Robert Brown and Son, aka The Sportsman Restoration Shop, in Sedro Woolley, Washington, a long way from Bill's home in Michigan. Bill made the trip, bought the Ford basket case and contracted with the Brown's to rebuild the body and fit it onto a Mercury chassis. The Brown's, (father and son) are noted Sportsman body builders. Bill had full confidence in their work.

Five years later, in July of 2007, the finished body was delivered to Bill's home workshop in Michigan, where with the help of friends the car was completed. NOS parts were used wherever possible. Bill did most of the work, except for the canvas top and upholstery. The body number is 146, initially built in July 1946.

In July of 2008 Bill took the newly finished car to the Early Ford V8 Club Grand National in Dearborn, Michigan. Where the car received the "*Dearborn Award*" and the "*Presidents Award*". In August of 2008 he took the car to the Meadow Book Concours d'Elegance event and received the "*Traditional Beauty Award*". In October he took the car to Hershey and received a AACA "*Junior 1st*" and the following year he received the AACA "*National Award*".

The Mercury Sportsman stands out at any event because of its rarity, and Bill's Greenfield Green car is an exceptional eye catcher, a testament to his tenacity.

The car that dared to be different!

Bill purchased a 1946 body skeleton from the Brown's Sportsman Shop in Sedro Woolley, WA. and contracted with them to make a new wood body, to be mounted on a Mercury chassis. **(shown here)** The body in primer is lowered onto the finished frame.

Wood framing components are fabricated and assembled from raw maple wood stock. Piece by piece the wood parts are dry fitted to the skeletal framing before gluing.

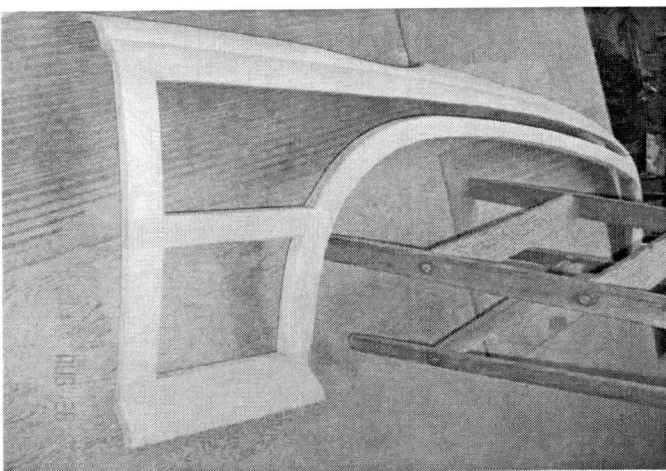

Photos from Bill Large Collection

53

Once the wood is dry fitted, finish sanding begins, before gluing and final assembly.

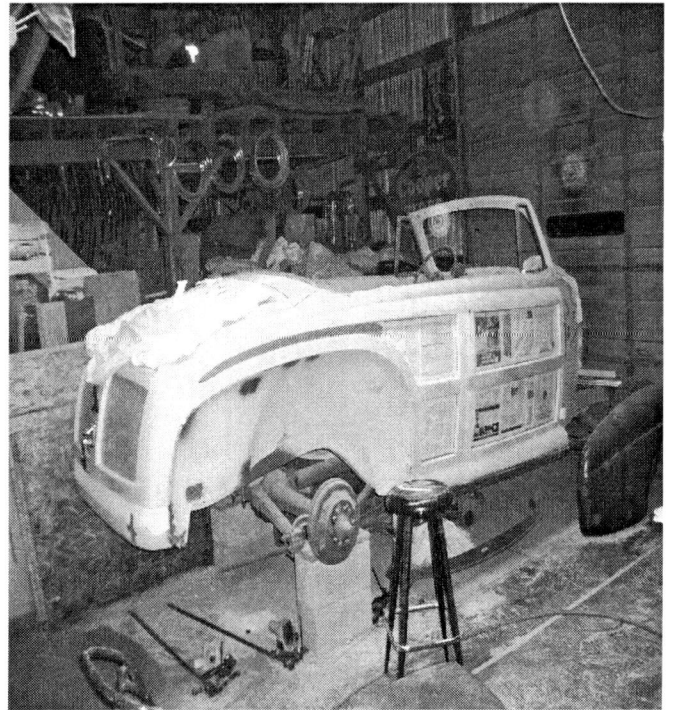

With the finish sanding completed the insert panels are installed and the wood is given a sealer coat before final varnishing, which will be done with wood on the car.

Photos from Bill Large

Bill Large inspects the finished body at the Brown's facility in Sedro Woolley, Washington, before being loaded for delivery to his home shop in Michigan for final assembly. While the body was being built, Bill was busy preparing the sheet metal front clip and the mechanics (engine, transmission, rear end, brakes, suspension, etc.)

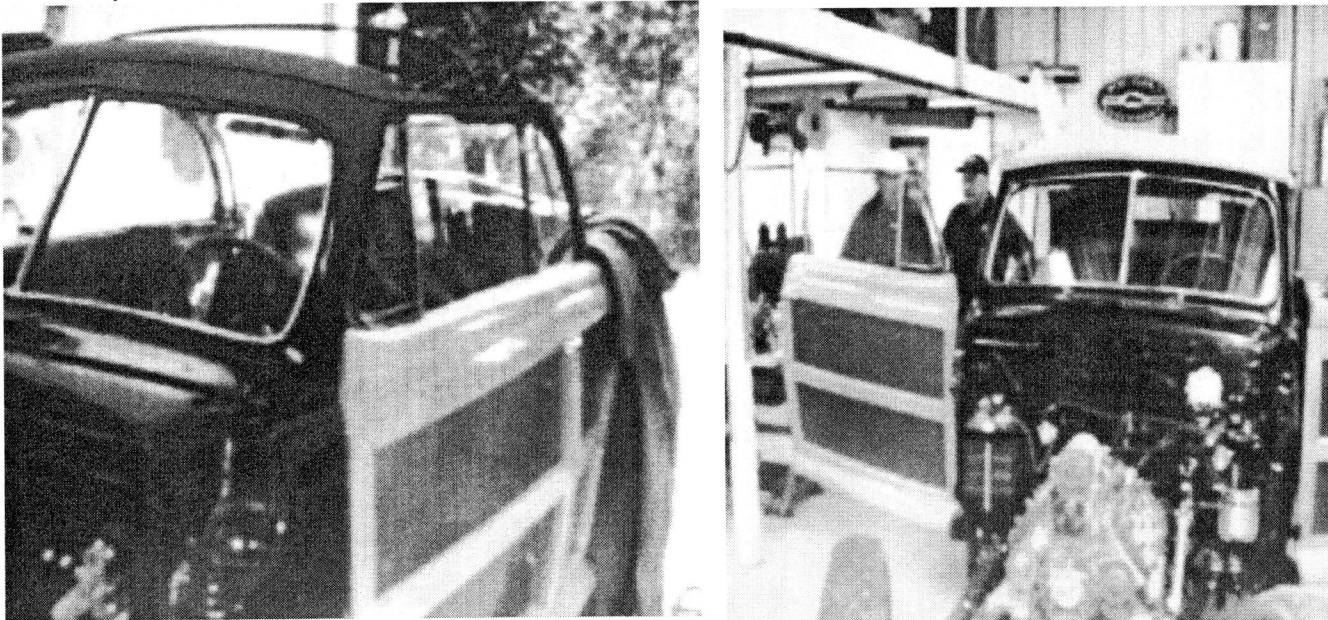

Once safely home in Bills shop the job of final assembly began almost immediately. A lot of the prep work was done, but there was still a lot to do and no time to waste.

Photos from Bill Large

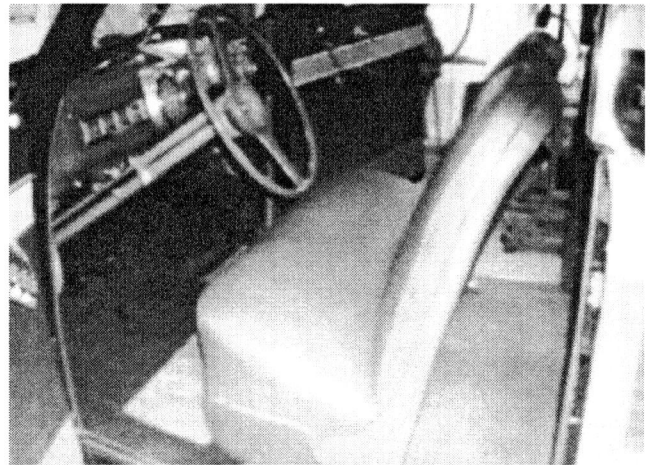

A new wood-grained dashboard was installed along with new refurbished gauges, speedometer and clock. Newly fabricated door panels and new tan leather upholstery and floor covering. Convertible top irons and hydraulics were rebuilt, a new tan top, rear window and weatherstripping was installed. The power window system was rebuilt Bill had to fabricate a lot of the parts himself as originals could not be found.

Photos from Bill Large

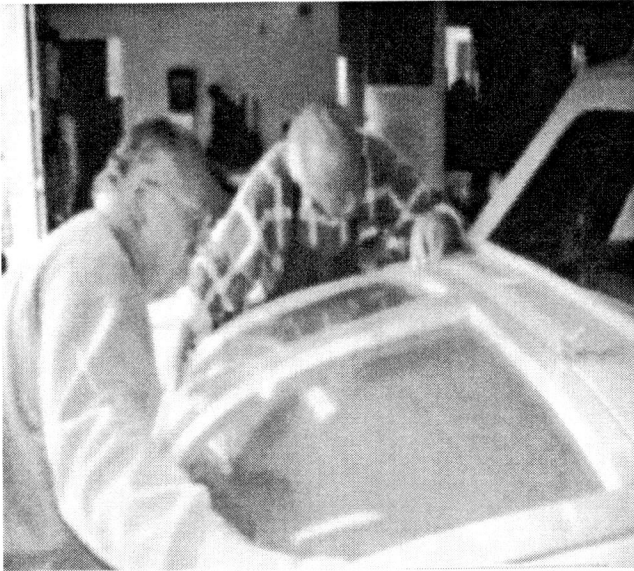

A lot of time was taken to carefully align the deck lid before hinges were installed

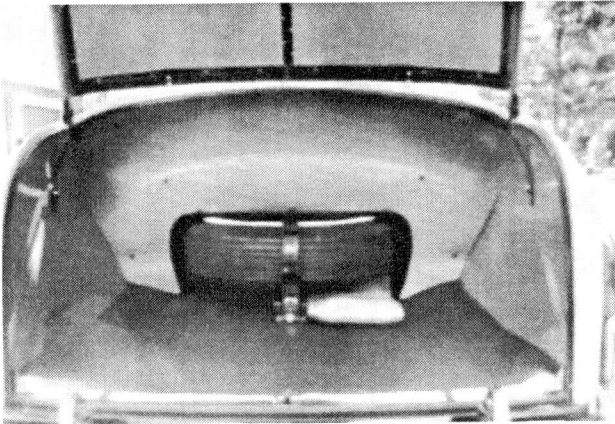

All the sheet metal was dry fitted, than removed and painted before final installation.

Photos from Bill Large

57

The Navy Blue 1946 Mercury Sportsman body number 382, part of the Nick Alexander Collection was sold at the Monterey 2009 RM Auction for a record setting $368,500.

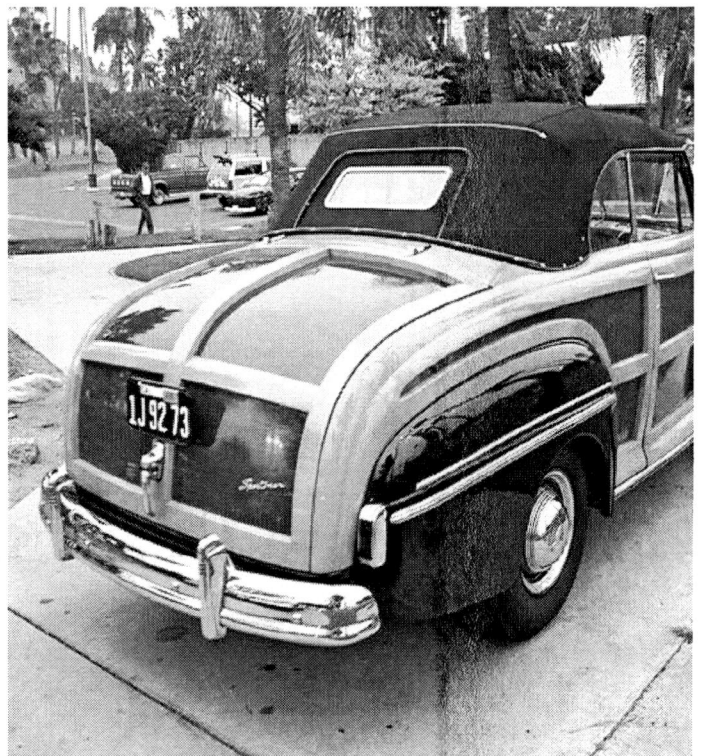

Photos from Nick Alexander Collection/RM Auctions and Yahoo.com

Barn find, Mercury Sportsman

Every car has a story, this is the story of the Navy Blue Mercury Sportsman. The existence of this particular car came to light at a local Chamber of Commerce car show in July 1973. While attending that show with my 1948 Chrysler Town & Country convertible I was approached by a young man who was curious as to the difficulty of restoring a wood bodied car. As I explained the skills necessary at the time to do the job he produced a photo of a derelict Sportsman, a Mercury Sportsman. My curiosity was peaked. This was the car he was considering restoring. Nothing more came of the conversation and we went our separate ways, but did exchange phone numbers.

A few weeks passed and I received a phone call. As it turned out the young man had decided against the project. He did not own the car, but if I was interested he would give me the mans name and work place; he lost the phone number.

And so began a little detective work (I'm sure this sounds all to familiar to most). The guy worked at a large manufacturing plant in Cleveland, Ohio, they ran three shifts at the plant. It took several calls at different times of the day, going through several departments before contact was made. As it turned out the guy did not own the car either, but did know the owners name and address. After some prodding I got the needed information. No phone number just an address.

Franklin Ledru Moody lived in Orwell, Ohio an hour drive east of Cleveland. A call to 411 directory assistance produced no listing. A road trip was in order. On a sunny Saturday in September I drove out to see Mr. Moody. The address was rural farmland. Fortunately Mr. Moody was at home and taken aback by my visit. Yes he had the old Mercury and he might be interested in selling. He showed me the car, which sat in an old dirt floor barn. It looked pretty sad, but I was hooked. I made an offer. Mr. Moody would think about it. After two more trips and some more haggling a deal was struck. On a cold gray day in October of 1973 the car was finally mine.

For several years prior I had been involved with Chrysler Town & Country's, so this was a new experience, but I was enthusiastic. Once the car was mine a full assessment was made. Most of the wood was intact, there was some collision damage to the left rear. The deck lid would have to be replaced, along with some of the wood framing. There was a lot of surface rust, the pot metal trim had corroded badly, the interior would have to be replaced. A lot of work had to be done, but it was all there. The motor was free and after a couple of weeks I did get it started, love those old Ford-Flat-Heads.

One of my first calls after acquiring the car was to Tom Garrett, founder of the Seventy-One Society. Tom and I had been in contact for some time, we had this mutual love of woodies. He was starting the Seventy-One Society and I was starting the Town & Country Owners Registry and had just written "Chrysler's Wonderful Woodie". Tom was surprised at my find and was very helpful, a great source of information. The body number is 382, built in September 1946.

After owning the car for a couple of years, and accumulating a number of parts, including a new deck lid, reality set in: I had too many projects and not enough time or the resources to finish them all. Without too much thought I sold the car to Tom Garrett, who I was confident would do it justice. Unfortunately Tom's untimely passing precluded any restoration on his part.

At some point the car was sold to Bruce Feight and subsequently purchased by Don Newby of Bondurant, Indiana. Newby did most of the restoration, and I believe changed the color. It was originally Navy Blue, which was changed to Maroon and spotlights added. I lost track of the car, but in March 1996 the Mercury was featured in an issue of Special Interest Autos, where I picked up its trail. According to the article by Tim Howley, Newby sold the car to Bob Dixon of Rockford, Illinois, from there it went to classic car dealer Bob Adams in Wisconsin, who sold it to Tom Dero, and some time later ended up with Curt Heaton. Once again the trail went cold. In 2009 the Mercury came up for auction as part of the Nick Alexander Collection. The RM Auction bio stated that Alexander acquired the car from Curt Heaton of del Mar California. I believe it was Alexander who changed the color back to the original Navy Blue and removed the spotlights.

The sale of the Mercury Sportsman at the Monterey RM Auction in 2009 set a record for Sportsman with a sale price of $368,500.

So that's the tale of the 1946 Navy Blue Mercury Sportsman, so far: as the end has yet to be written. I'm sure one day we'll hear more about this special car.

Don Narus

After spending the morning getting the Blue Merc out of the old barn I stopped and took some time to hose off a couple of decades of accumulation of dirt, before heading home and putting the car safely away in my garage. It had been a long day.

Photos by the author from David Kuffel Collection

The original Red leather interior was dirty and moldy but complete and intact. Accessories include: electric clock, radio and heater. The basket weave door panel strip was in very good shape. The floor mats and carpeting in need of replacement.

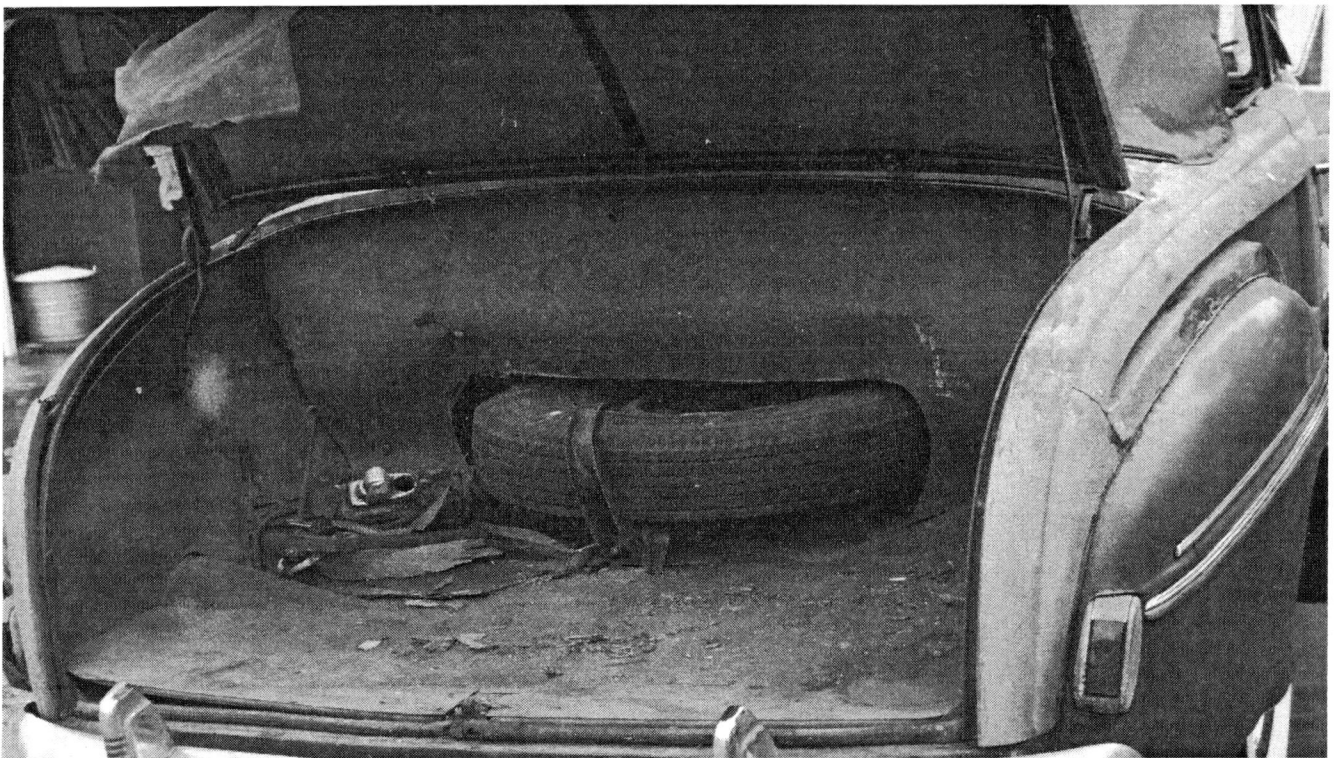

The trunk was intact but the deck lid was badly damaged and needing replacement. The left quarter, tail light, rear fender, wood framing and bumper were damaged. Pieces of the deck lid and deck lock assembly are seen in the left corner of the trunk

Photos by the author from Dave Kuffel Collection

The 1946 Mercury Sportsman as restored by Don Newby. Original color changed to Dynamic Maroon code M-3989. Spotlights, side view mirrors and bumper wings were added. Antenna moved to passenger side. Buffalo Horns grille guard was retained.

The color was changed back to its original Navy Blue code M-3982. The spotlights, side view mirrors, bumper wing guards and Buffalo Horns grille guard were removed. The car is as original, including black wall tires, as it would have been in 1946.

Photos from RM Auctions and Hemmings Motor News/David Gooly

1946 4 Door Town Sedan
Body Type 73

1946 Tudor Sedan
Body Type 70

1946 Sport Convertible Coupe
Body Type 71

1946 Convertible Club Coupe
Body Type 76

1946 Sedan Coupe
Body Type 72

1946 Station Wagon
Body Type 79

1947-48 Station Wagon
Body Type 79

1947-48 4 Door Town Sedan
Body Type 73

1947-48 Sedan Coupe
Body Type 72

1947-48 Convertible Club Coupe
Body Type 76

1946 in Dark Slate Gray, code M-3981, Black top, Red piping, "A" wood pattern.
Photos from conceptcarz.com and Dave Kuffel Collection

Late 1947, 799A1934335 with "C" pattern wood. Sold at auction for $162,250 in 2009

Early 1947, 799A1691621 with "B" pattern wood. Sold at auction for $220,000. in 2009

Photo from Nick Alexander Collection/RM Auctions

Chapter Two
1947

1947 was a bit convoluted. To start with, all serial numbers beginning in January, for all Ford models were given a 799A prefix and were sold as 1947 models. However the early cars still had 1946 sheet metal trim, with the "A" pattern bodies and were considered by Ford to be 1946 models. In late February, early March the wood pattern was changed to "B", but still carried the 1946 sheet metal trim and were also considered to be 1946 cars even though they had the 1947 serial numbers.

The real styling change came in April. The "B" pattern was dropped and the"C" pattern was introduced, along with changes to the grille and dashboard gauges. All cars produced after April 1, 1947 had the 1947 trim, except for eleven cars which were assembled with the 1946 trim as follows: four in Long Beach, California, six in Richmond, California and one in Dearborn, Michigan.

Most 1947 Sportsman have the "B" pattern wood with the 1947 sheet metal trim. The sheet metal trim was the most recognizable change: the parking lights were moved to below the headlights and were no longer rectangle. The red stripes on the horizontal grille bars were removed along with the Special Deluxe script on the left front fender. A new emblem was added to just above the center Ford grille script, which designated Super Deluxe with a number 8 which indicated eight cylinder. A new hood ornament with a plastic insert replaced the solid chrome one of 1946, however although the 1946 hood ornament was dropped the new one was not added until July. So the early 1947 models, those manufactured after April 1st, and before July 1st, did not have a hood ornament.

1947 Maize Yellow paint code 14229, looks right at home in your back yard or at the shore. Options include: White Walls, Wheel discs and wheel rings, End bumper guards, fog lights radio, heater and drivers side view mirror. Red interior with black top.

Photos from owner Dave Kuffle

Spotlights, fog lights, swan neck side view mirrors, windshield mount antenna, bumper wings, white wall tires, wheel trim rings are all options. Pheasant Red, code 14230

1947 with "B" body wood, with optional fog lights, spotlight, dual side view mirrors. fender mounted antenna, white wall tires and wheel trim rings. Black, code M-1724.

Photos from yahoo.com pics

(upper photo) 1947 Tucson Tan, code 14227 **(lower)** Greenfield Green code M-3990.

Photos from Rex Gray and the Browns

There was great attention to detail paid in the restoration of this 1947 Sportsman.

Photos from Hyman Ltd Classic Cars

Dual spotlights, dual swan neck side view mirrors, fog lights and bumper wings, all are authorized options that were available for the Ford Sportsman in 1947.

Tan leather upholstery, shown here, was one of two options, the other was Red.

The wonder-bar radio and electric clock were usually found in the Sportsman.

Photos from Hyman Ltd Classic cars

The Tan top, with small glass window was one of two colors available, the other; Black

Nicely restored 1947 Ford Sportsman, painted Modern Blue. code M-3987.

Photos from Hyman Ltd Classic Cars

Original '47

Gerald Greenfield has been collecting cars for many years and during that time has had an eclectic collection of classic cars; from a 1934 Packard V12 Victoria convertible which won Best in Class at the Pebble Beach Concourse, to a impeccable 1941 Town & Country that set an auction sales record, to a incredible Ford GT. But his favorite car is the Ford Sportsman.

He purchased his first Sportsman in 1988. A Tucson Tan 1946. It was the first Sportsman restored by Robert J. Brown and Son of Sedor-Woolley, Washington. Since than they have become the definitive Sportsman Restoration and Body Building Shop.

In 1990 Gerald sold his '46 and immediately regretted the sale. He promised himself that he would get another Sportsman. Ten years and a number of fabulous classics later the urge to get that replacement Sportsman finally took hold. The first thing he did was place wanted ads in collector and club publications.

In March of 2000 he received a reply to his ad and found himself heading for San Diego to check out an original 1947 with forty-one thousand original miles. The car was Barcelona Blue (dark blue), the paint was thin in spots but it had excellent wood and chrome. The top needed replacing and the interior leather stitching needed attention. Overall it was a great car. He made an offer, but Scott, the owner, could not come to an agreement. Gerald returned home disappointed and once again renewed his quest.

In August 2001 Gerald purchased his second Sportsman, a restored 1947, Maroon with Red leather. The car was nicely restored, but the wood was not as nice as the Blue original. Six months after the purchase he received a call from Scott, who finally agreed to accept his offer. Gerald was now the proud owner of two Ford Sportsman.

He immediately sold the restored '47 and concentrated on the original. First he carefully detailed the paint. The wood was perfect and needed nothing. The front seat leather was not presentable, so vintage seat covers were purchased. The original Black top with Red piping, was replaced with a dark Blue top, its not original but Gerald liked it. He drove it one thousand miles per year for the next seven years. In November of 2009 he sold the car to a guy in Florida who was in the import/export business and believes the car was shipped to Brazil.

The original 1947 Barcelona Blue, paint code 14221, had 41,000 original miles at the time of purchase. Paint, chrome, wood, and optional rear fender skirts are all original.

Photos from owner Gerald Greenfield

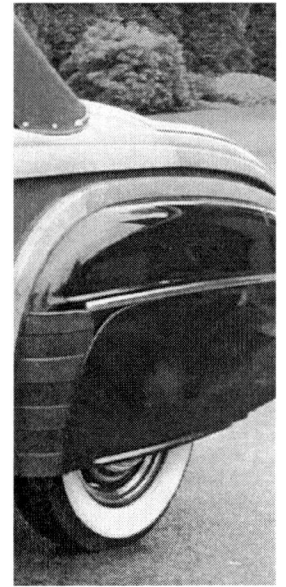

The bumper wings, grille guard and fog lights are original. The original paint, thin in spots was carefully detailed. The original wood was perfect and needed nothing.

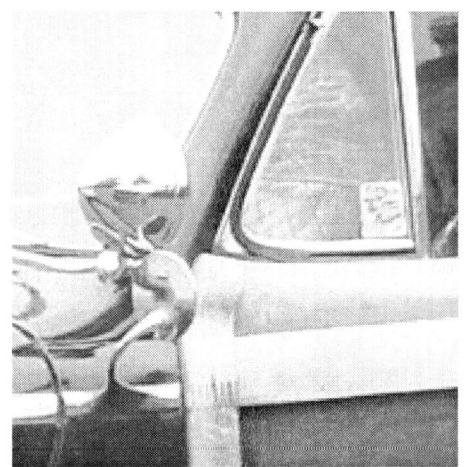

The hood ornament is a flying lady, of sorts, with her legs in a "V" holding a number 8. Gerald found it at Hershey. All the other accessories are original to the car.

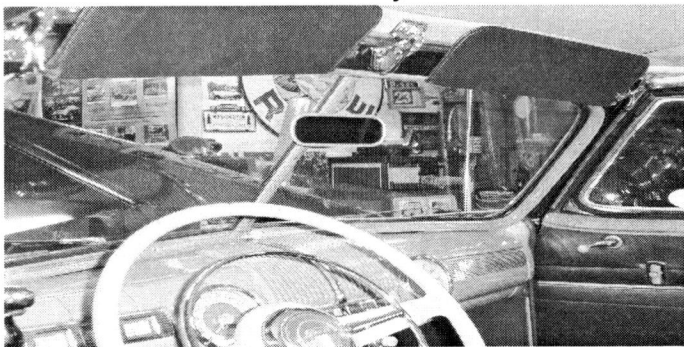

The interior is original. The front seats are protected with vintage seat covers.

Photos are from Gerald Greenfield

(left), 1946 grill with red pin stripes and "Special Deluxe" front fender script.**(right),** new 1947-1948 grille, sans red pin stripes, new round parking lights and bumper guards.

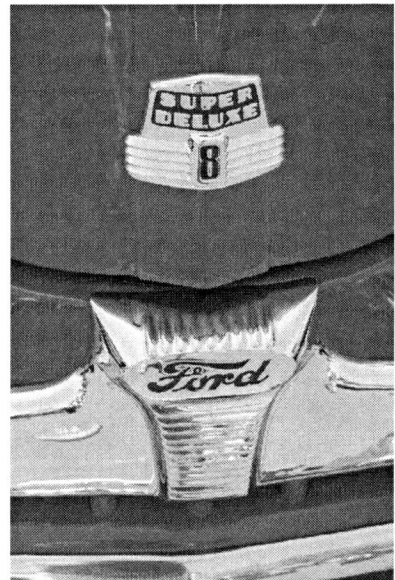

(left) The 1946 nose script in red. **(center),** the "Bull Nose" 1947 models built after April 1st and before July 1947. **(right),** blue nose script and new Special Deluxe badge, all models built after July 1, 1947 and though 1948. Most common Sportsman model.

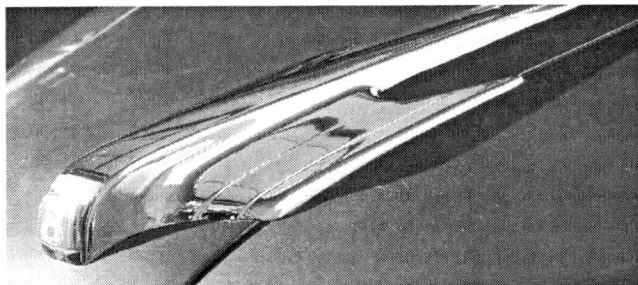

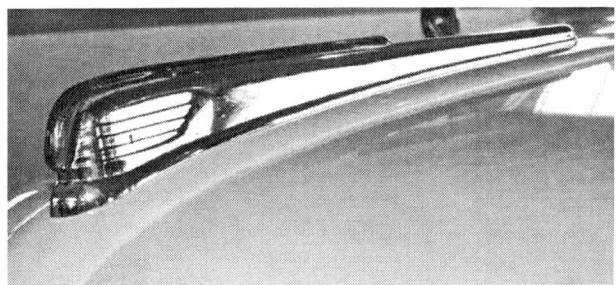

(left), the 1946 hood ornament. The 8 indicates eight cylinder. **(right),** the new 1947-1948 hood ornament, More streamlined with a blue plastic insert.

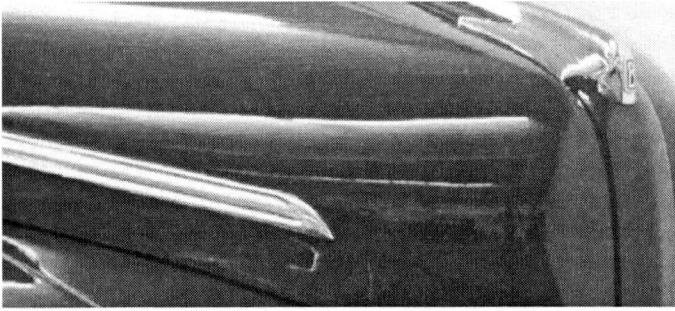

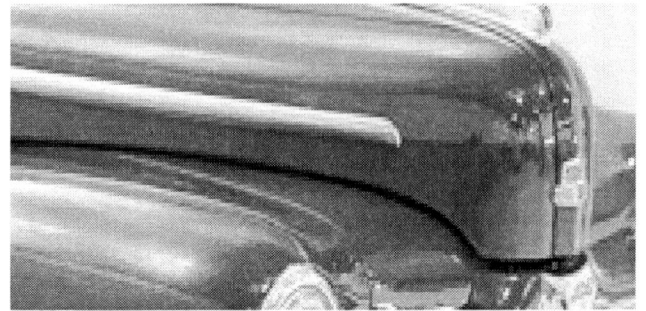

Molding trim changed, grooved in 1946 **(left)** it was now smooth in 1947 **(right)**.

Hub caps and wheel rings changed. The 1946 **(left)** hub cap had block letter FORD with accent strips highlighted in red. The wheel ring had fine groves. In 1947 **(right)** the hub caps had block FORD highlighted in blue. The wheel ring had a bold grove.

In 1946 **(left)** the rocker molding stopped at the edge of the front fender. In 1947**(right)** the rocker molding wrapped around the fender, like the 1946 Mercury **(see inset).**

Photos from St. Louis Car Museum. Hyman Lts, Rm Auction, Gerald Greenfield

The quest for perfection

Henry Miller doesn't remember the name of the movie or the actors, but he did remember the car, a Sportsman. This was in the early 1970's. His passion for the Sportsman began with that movie poster. Henry was an auto mechanic in South Vancouver, Canada. He placed wanted ads in U.S. Collector Car magazines. He patiently waited and after three years, September 1975, he got a reply, A guy in Orange Country California had a original 1947 with 78,000 miles with very good wood. Henry hooked up his trailer and drove to California to buy the car, and thus began the quest for perfection.

Henry dismantled the complete car, bolt by bolt, and over the next thirty-three years, he researched. Making sure every nut and bolt was exactly correct as Ford had originally built it. Every part of the car was completely rebuilt using only genuine Ford parts correct for the year 1947. He did all the work himself, except for the convertible top and leather upholstery. He never lost focus.

In 2008 he took the completed car to Dearborn, Michigan for the Early Ford V8 Grand National. He scored 998 points out of a possible 1,000 and received the prestigious *"Dearborn Award"* for the best restoration. Few cars come close to that score. Henry Miller had achieved his goal of "perfection"!

Photo by Alyn Edwards Canadian News Service

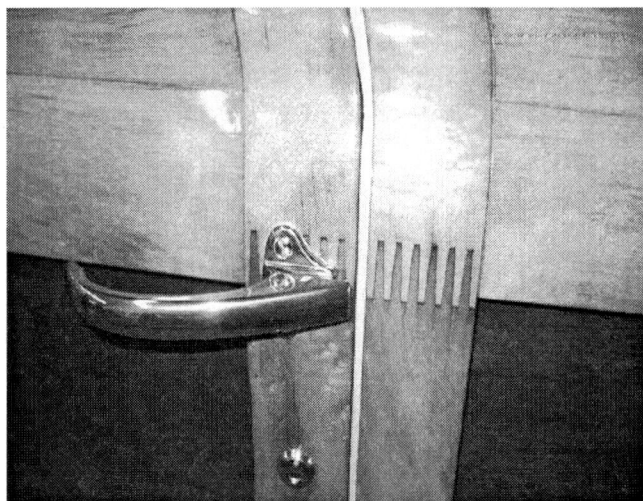

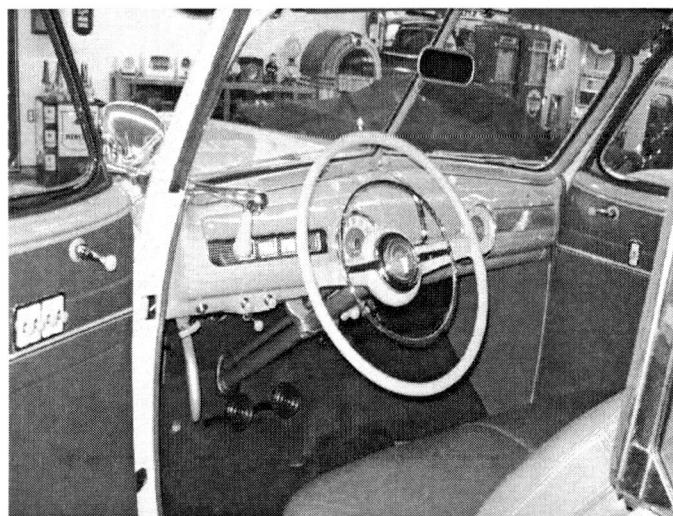

Henry Millers Maize Yellow, code 14229, Sportsman is an early 1947,(bull nose) with the "B" pattern wood and using front and rear 1946 bumpers. It was completely taken apart and re-done by Henry over a 33 year period. There is no doubt it is "perfect".

Photos by Alyn Edwards Canadian News Service

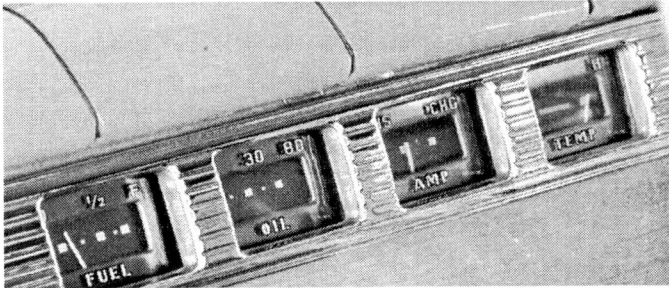

Among the changes for 1947 included the dashboard trim and gauge faces. **1946 left, 1947 right.** The red pin stripe was removed from the plastic, the Ford script was removed from the glove box and gauge faces changed from black to silver.

The 1946 dashboard on top, the 19478-48 on the bottom, essentially the same, but different. <u>Note:</u> the horn button also changed in 1947, as did the steering wheel.

Photos from various sources

81

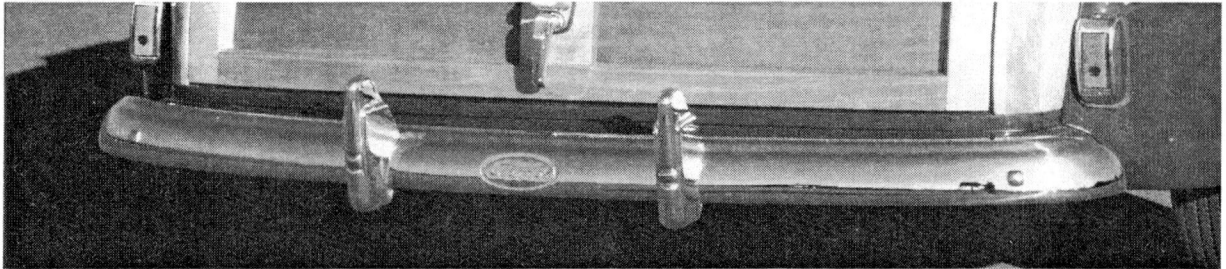

The 1946 Ford front bumper **(upper)** and the rear bumper **(lower)** with script.

The 1947-48 Ford front bumper **(upper)** and the rear bumper **(lower)** no script.

The 1946 Mercury front bumper **(upper)** and the rear bumper **(lower).**

Note: If you are into details, you may notice that the 1946 bumper guards both Ford and Mercury are very similar to the 1950 Ford.

Photos from various sources

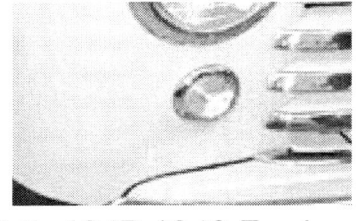

Parking lights: **(left)**, 1946 Mercury. **(center)**, 1946 Ford. **(right)**, 1947-1948 Ford.

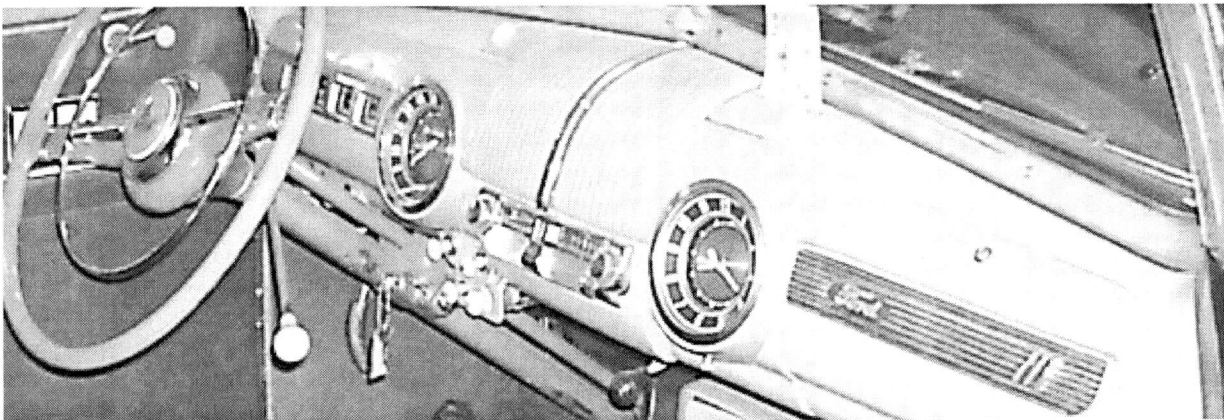

Dashboards: **(top)**, 1946 Mercury. **(center)**, 1946 Ford. **(bottom)**, 1947-1948 Ford.

Photos from Rex Gray, Gene Hetland and various sources

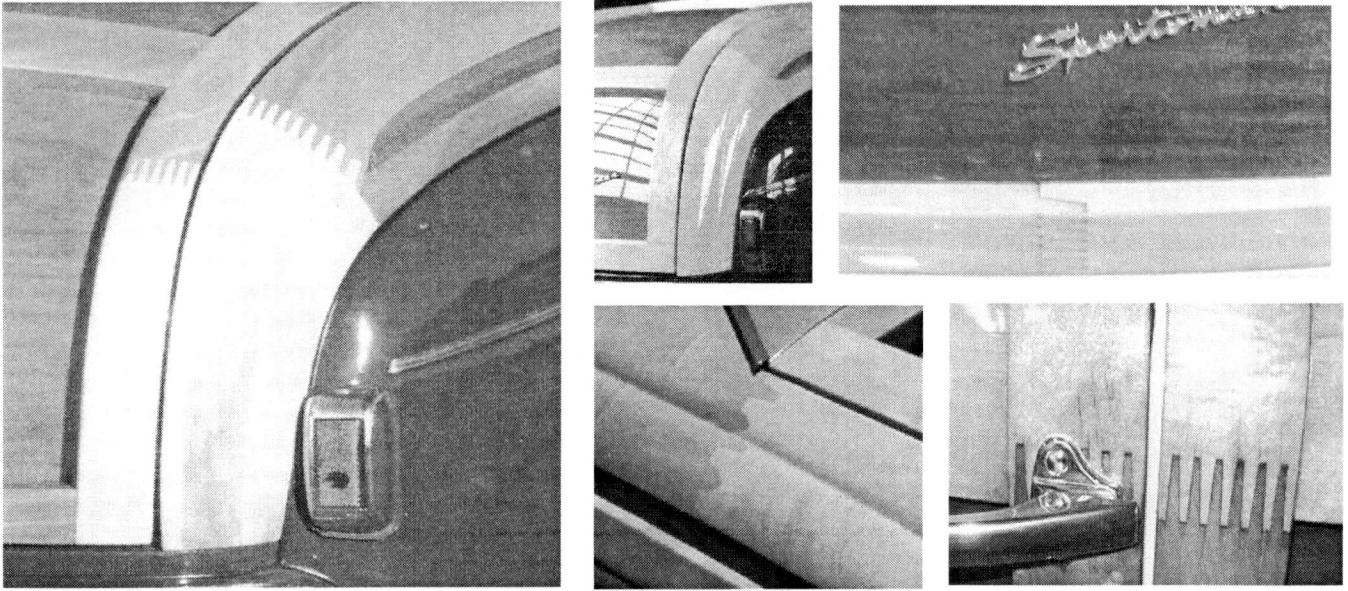

Ford used a various finger, tenon and lap joints to join small pieces of Maple framing.

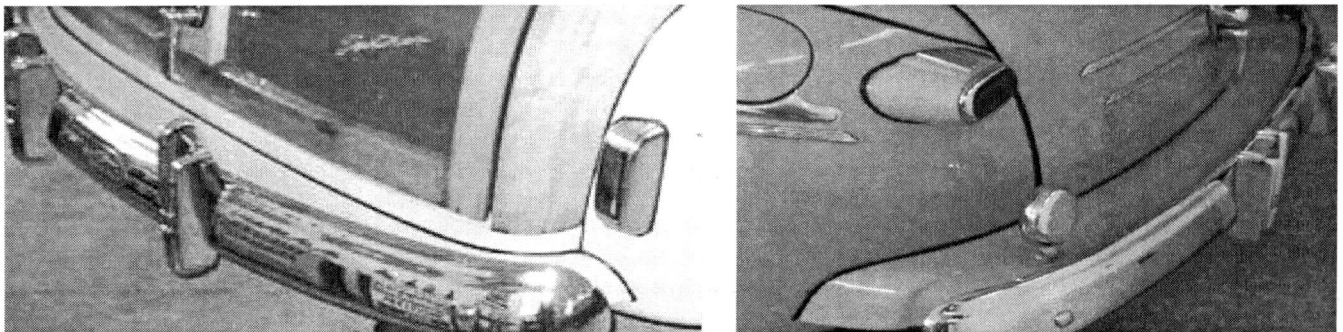

(left), the Sportsman rear splash pan is unique to the Sportsman, not interchangeable with the steel body convertible **(right),** due to rear fender configuration.

Photos from Dave Kuffel, Terry Johnson, Ford Motor Archives, Alyn Edwards and various sources

Available accessories included: a sun visor vanity mirror and a flow-thru heater.

The hydraulic windows were taken from the Lincoln, the color of the switch was changed from Dark Maroon to Ivory. **(left),** Mercury switches were so mounted that they interrupted the trim. **(right),** Ford switches were mounted above the trim.

Mercury **(left),** Ford **(right),** single switches were mounted on the passenger door and the rear quarter trim panels. Vent windows were operated by a crank.

Photos from Dave Kuffel, Bill Large, Mike DeViriendt, Gerald Greenfield and Hyman Ltd

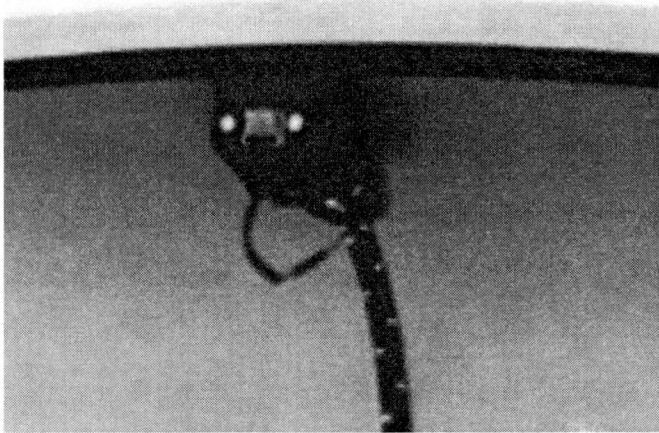

Inside and out, the rear deck locking mechanism, it also incorporated a license lamp.

Outside and inside. A single plywood panel, maple framing. Cardboard panel liner.

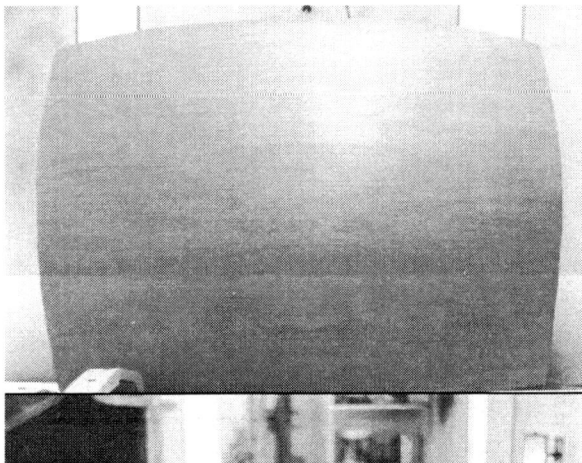

Left, a single pressure bent Mahogany plywood panel fitted into a Maple frame, **right,** completed the deck lid. This is the only structural wood part of the Sportsman.

Photos from Dave Kuffel and Bill Large Collections

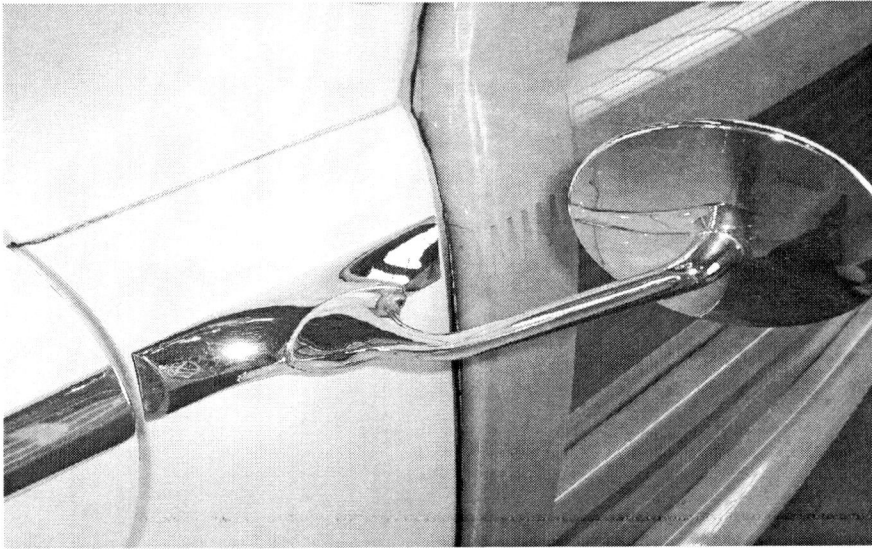

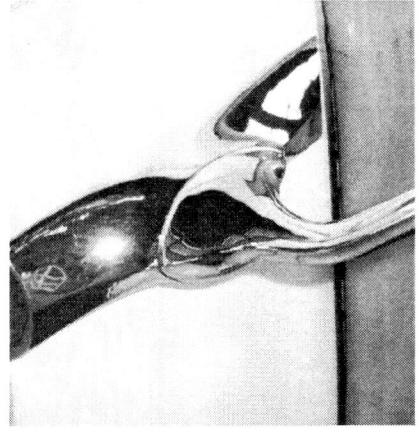

Straight neck side view mirror, a popular Ford and Mercury accessory.

Steering wheels: **(left),** 1946 Ford, **(center),** 1947-48 Ford, **(right),** 1946 Mercury.

Wing guards: (le**ft),** 1946 Mercury, **(right),** 1946-1947-1948 Ford. Both bolted outside.

Photos from Dave Kuffel Collection, and various internet sources

This 1947 body number 2224, was built in May 1947. Paint color is Pheasant Red Code 14230. Wood frame is original but the insert panels have been replaced. Original Red leather interior and a new Black top with Red piping, as the original.

Photos by owner Gene Hetland

LIMITED EDITION 1948 FORD SPORTSMAN

Ford's stunning land yacht sets sail – for a very limited time!

(continued from inside)

Production ends forever 12/31/08!

Your V-8 is waiting!

Ford's self-proclaimed "great V-8" lies under the hood of the Danbury Mint's *Limited Edition 1948 Ford Sportsman*. Producing 100hp from 239.4 cubic inches, this legendary flathead engine was a favorite among Big Three buyers who wanted some "oomph" in their rides. The undercarriage components are just as perfect. In the trunk, you'll find the spare tire/wheel assembly. Ford built the Sportsman to mesmerize potential customers; we think that enchantment has carried over quite well into our replica! So will you!

What's that sound... a clock ticking?

Just over two dozen of these beauties ever saw the light of day in 1948. There will be more of the Danbury Mint's version available, but production will be strictly limited, so don't wait to order. After <u>December 31, 2008 we will end production</u> of this museum-quality replica *forever*. This stunning die-cast model is priced at a modest $149 plus $9 total shipping and service, payable in four monthly installments of $39.50. There is absolutely no risk involved. If you wish to return your replica to us for any reason, you may do so within 30 days for replacement or full refund. Don't let this one get away; order today!

The Danbury Mint Brochure

Chapter Three
1948

The last month of Ford Sportsman production was November 1947. During that month only 28 cars were assembled. All of these units were given the serial number prefix of 899A- and designated 1948 models. They were unchanged from 1947. All used the "C" pattern wood bodies. It's interesting to note that all the 1948 models were built in November 1947 and all were sold prior to January 1948.

During the Sportsman's short run there are several interesting notes: from the total production of 3,692, not counting the original prototype, seventy-six were exported, four with right hand drive. There were no six cylinder models. Although 3,692 cars were assembled, a total of 3,725 bodies were actually produced. 33 bodies are unaccounted for. It is speculated that these were either used as replacements or simply scraped during quality control inspections. But there is no written evidence of either.

Elbert Marston purchased the Maize Yellow 1948 Sportsman, serial number 899A-2064609, body number 3725 (recorded as the last Sportsman produced) on December 25, 1947 from Pearson Ford in San Diego, California. A Christmas gift for his wife Georgia, a school teacher. Prior to her retirement she drove the car daily for twenty years. It has been across country twice. In the twenty years of daily driving the top was replaced twice, the radiator replaced once. After her retirement the car was driven sparsely, it had accumulated 58,000 miles. On November 3, 1983 the car was stolen right from Mrs. Marston's garage, without a clue. Years later the car showed up in Tucson, Arizona. Bob Evert purchased the car only to find out it was stolen, he ended up paying twice for the Sportsman. He had to re-purchase the car from its rightful owner. Later Bob sold the car to Ty Froemke of California who did a frame off total restoration. Ultimately the car ended up with Curt Heaton of Corona Del Mar, California. Heaton sold the '48 along with a rare Mercury Sportsman to famed woodie collector Nick Alexander. It sold at auction in 2009.

The last Sportsman 1948 Maize Yellow, body 3725 sold at auction $236,500 in 2009.
The 1948 Maize yellow Sportsman sits in the staging area awaiting auction in 2009

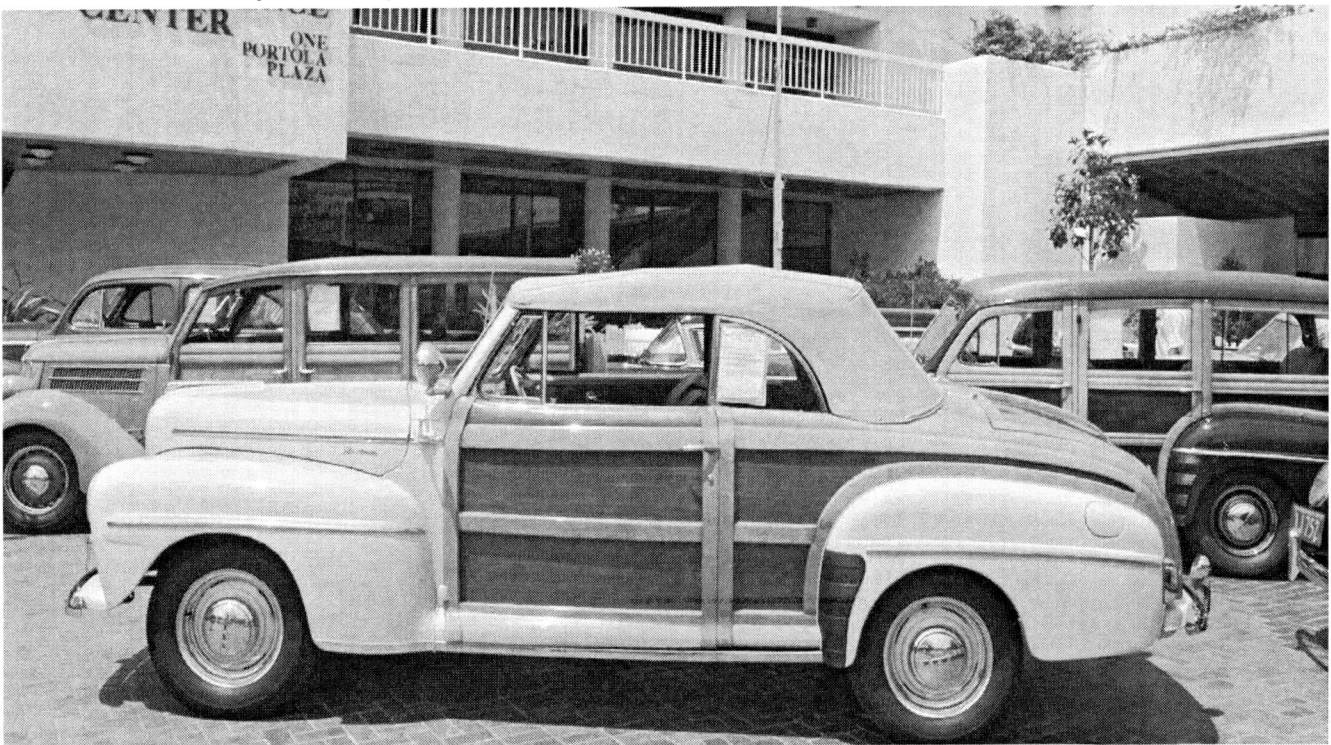

Photos from Alexander Collection/RM Auctions and conceptcarz.com

The 1948, the last Sportsman as seen at the Ameila Island Concourse d'Elegance. During the first twenty years it was driven daily and across the country twice accumulating 58, 000 miles before being sold by its original owner. Only 28 were built.

Even though white wall tires were available in 1948 they were not always chosen as an option. Because of its placement, I suspect the spotlight was dealer installed. The side view mirror is straight arm, not swan. Red leather was one of three choices

Photos from conceptcarz.com

Minor differences between 1946 and the 1947-48 included the fender trim, In 1946 it sat above the fender crease and wrapped around. Hub caps were different, the 1946 models (**right**) used a red highlighted block Ford, the 1947-48 was highlighted blue.

Photos from various sources

This original 1948 two owner car was stripped down to the bones and re-furbished like new by Classic Showcase; retaining the original color Midland Maroon, code 14202. New tan top was installed as original, and the original interior was retained. All the options: spotlights, fog lights, bumper wings are original to the car. Note: the missing DeLuxe 8 cylinder hood nose badge. This would normally indicate that the car had a six cylinder engine, however there is no record of any six cylinder Sportsman built.

The mechanics as well as the body and paint were completely re-done to as new.

Photos from Classic Showcase

With only 28 Sportsman built for 1948, few have survived, they are among the rarest

of Ford Sportsman. Most Sportsman were delivered with many accessory options.

Photos from the internet

1946-47-48 Ford Sportsman
Model 71

Wheelbase:114 inches Engine:100hp V-8 Transmission: 3-speed manual

Model	Price	Built
Sportsman Convertible Coupe	1946- $1,982.	1209
	1947- 2,282.	2250
	1948- 2,282.	28

1946 Mercury Sportsman
Model 71

Wheelbase:118 inches   Engine:100hp V-8 Transmission: 3-speed manual

Model	Price	Built
Sportsman Convertible Coupe	1946- $2.209.	205

Body Paint Colors

Black	M-1724 *	Barcelona Blue	14221**
Greenfield Green	M-3990 *	Monsoon Maroon	14222**
Navy Blue	M-3982 *	Glade Green	14223**
Botsford Blue	M-3983 *	Feather Gray	14224**
Modern Blue	M-3987 *	Blue Gray	14225**
Dynamic Maroon	M-3989 *	Tucson Tan	14227**
Dark Slate Gray	M-3981 *	Maize Yellow	14229**
Silver Sand	M-3992 *	Pheasant Red	14230**
Willow Green	M-14140*	Midland Maroon	14202^^
Light Moonstone	M-3981 *	Shoal Green Gray	14228^^
		Strato Blue	14201^^

Canvas Top	Interior
Black (Red piping-'46 Only)	Red Leather
Tan (match piping-'47-'48)	Tan Leather
	Blue Gray Leather

*1946 **1947 ^^1948 Spec information from Standard Catalog of Ford by John Gunnell,& Seventy-one Society

1946 Sportsman Coupe Type 71

1946 Super DeLuxe Sedan Coupe
Type 72-B

1946 Super DeLuxe Fordor Sedan Type 73-B
Type 73-A (DeLuxe)

1946 Super DeLuxe Tudor Sedan
Type 70-B   Type 70-A (DeLuxe)

1946 DeLuxe (5 Window) Coupe Type 77-A
Type 77-B (Super DeLuxe)

1946 Super DeLuxe Station Wagon Type 79-B

1946 Super DeLuxe Convertible Club Coupe
Type 76

1947-48 Super DeLuxe Station Wagon
Type 79-B

1947 Sportsman Coupe Type 71

1947-48 Super DeLuxe Sedan Coupe
Type 72-B

1947-48 Super DeLuxe Convertible Club Coupe
Type 76

1947-48 DeLuxe Tudor Sedan Type 70-A
Type 70-B (Super DeLuxe)

1947-48 DeLuxe (5 Window) Coupe Type 77-A
Type 77-B (Super DeLuxe)

The competition

When it came to post World War II woodies, Chrysler was the most ambitious. No less than five models were proposed: a 4-door Sedan, a 2-door Brougham Sedan, a 2-door Hardtop Coupe, A Convertible and a Roadster. However the complexity of building the post-war Town & Country dashed that ambition. In the end only the Convertible and the 4-door Sedan actually went into production, although six Hardtop Coupes were actually built. Had Chrysler adopted the Ford method of construction, perhaps the Hardtop and Roadster could have reached full production.

The Chrysler Town & Country Convertible did not compete head to head with Ford, it was aimed at a different market. The affluent, upscale market, while Ford wanted to appeal to the much larger mid-range or lower end market. Neither Ford or Chrysler sold their woodie convertible in great numbers (Ford sold a total of 3,487 for 1946-48. Chrysler did somewhat better at 8,375 for the same period). Numbers did not tell the whole story, since the amount of dealer traffic that each car generated was priceless.

In comparison: each car (Ford and Chrysler) had eight cylinder engines. Ford had a 100hp V8, while Chrysler had a 135hp In-line 8. Ford had a three speed manual transmission while Chrysler had a semi-automatic "Fluid Drive". Both offered power operated tops. Ford's wheelbase was 114 inches (Mercury 118 inches) compared to Chrysler's 127-1/2 inches. In 1946 the Ford sold for $1,982. and the Chrysler sold for $2,725.

Chevrolet was another story. There was a model called the Country Club which Chevrolet officially disavowed, although it was exclusively marketed through authorized Chevrolet dealers. The Country Club was a "woodie" kit sold and installed by the dealer. It was available as a Aero Sedan, a Club Coupe and a Convertible. The wood was applied directly over the sheet metal.

The framing was probably Oak with veneer Mahogany panels. Highly varnished and requiring the same maintenance as the Ford and Chrysler. It sold for $149.50 plus installation. Unofficially 100 were sold; it was attractive.

Maybe, just maybe, had Ford and Chrysler adopted the same technique as that of the Country Club there would have been more Sportsman and T&C's on the road. But then again they wouldn't be a true "Woodie".

Chrysler

The Chrysler Town & Country was part of the luxury car market and did not really compete with Ford head to head. Now, had this been a Plymouth it would be a different story. The 1946-48 T&C was more complicated to build. It was the highest priced car in Chrysler's line up, production was low, but all thing's considered sold well.

Photos from the authors collection

1947 Saturday Evening Post Town & Country ad by famed artist John Clymer

From the authors collection

Chevrolet

The Cabriolet Custom Country Club . . . Impressive in any company, the Cabriolet Custom Country Club has a new beauty that accents the contrast of varied body and top colors.

The Newest Smartest "Look" in Cars

THE NEW
CUSTOM COUNTRY CLUB

NEW SMARTNESS — The Custom Country Club is a line of three Chevrolet models that are completely new in the smartness and fresh appearance of their wood-panelled exterior design.

QUALITY — PERMANENCE — The Custom Country Club is designed of choicest materials—beautifully-finished long-grained hardwoods, and new, permanent, patented mahogany-grained panelling—built to last the lifetime of your car.

SAFETY AND COMFORT — The Custom Country Club gives you the warmth of wood finishes added to all the complete safety, built-in comfort, and cushioned quietness of today's finest steel body construction.

AVAILABLE NOW — The Custom Country Club is available now from your Chevrolet dealer at slight extra cost on three models; The Aero-sedan Custom Country Club, the Cabriolet Custom Country Club and the Custom Country Club Coupe.

ENGINEERED ENTERPRISES INC.   •   1029 FISHER BLDG.   •   DETROIT 2, MICH.   •   PHONE TRINITY 3-4350

"Portions of materials contained herein have been reprinted with permission of General Motors Corporation, Service Operations." License 0710896

Shown above is the Country Club brochure. The Country Club woodie kit was offered exclusively through, and installed by authorized Chevrolet Dealers. The number of kits

sold is estimated at 100. The Country Club was not officially recognized by Chevrolet although, ironically, the company that made the kit, Engineered Enterprises had their headquarters in the Fisher Bldg, (GM HQ) in downtown Detroit, Michigan.

Material from the authors collection

Odds and Ends

The lure of a "woodie" is evident in the three examples covered here. If you can't find one, or you want something unique. Build it! That's exactly what the owners of our examples did.

First is the so-called Mercury Sportsman Sedan. The owner of this car apparently figured that Ford should have built a Mercury "Woodie" sedan, after all Chrysler built one, Nash built one, Packard built one, so why not Ford. And wouldn't Mercury have made a good choice. The "Woodie"style chosen by the owner was similar to the Nash Suburban. Great care was taken to insure a quality build, from the design, to the choice of wood, to the application. The quality is apparent. The finished product, a 1947 Mercury Sportsman Sedan, looks like something that could very well have been built by Ford Motor Company. Maybe they should have given it a shot. It would have been easier to built then the Sportsman convertible or the station wagon.

Next, we have the custom built, do-it-yourself 1948 Ford Sportsman. The owner of this car probably liked the Sportsman so much that he turned his stock convertible into a "Woodie" Sportsman. Easier and cheaper than trying to find the real thing. Hey why not, what's the big deal, it's just a little wood stuck to a metal body. What's interesting is how the owner figured he could pull this off and still keep the metal body. I'm speculating that what he had to work from were photographs of the real thing. The framing is thin, the insert panels may be painted on or a decal. There are no finger joints, nothing sophisticated, it appears that all work was done by hand, using hand tools and decently executed. This one I find intriguing.

Lastly, we have the 1940 Ford "Woodie" convertible. This one is very unique. It appears that all the wood is structural. It is an exercise in wood sculpturing. A lot of time and effort went into this build and required a considerable amount of talent. A close look at the details gives you some indication as to the craftsmanship that went into this car. Whether you like it or hate it you have to admire the workmanship. Strictly from a "Woodie" point of view the car hits the mark, from a strictly stock point of view, not so much. I'm sure that wherever this car is shown it attracts attention, a crowd pleaser.

1947 Mercury Sportsman Sedan

The 1947 Mercury Sedan "Woodie" (or Spoprtsman Sedan if you like) was built a lot like the 1946-48 Nash Suburban. No part of the steel body was removed, the wood was laid over the steel panel and fastened from the inside. The roof rack was similar to the one used on the 1941 Chrysler T&C Sedan. The interior was upholstered in vinyl, door panels and rear quarter panels, were made from Mahogany veneered plywood.

Photos from Yahoo.com images

(left) The deck lid design was more like Ford and Chrysler than Nash **(right)**.

From the side the similarities between the Mercury **(left)** and the Nash **(right)** are evident. The difference was in the wood used. The Nash used Ash as did Chrysler. The Mercury appears to have used Maple or Birch staying true to Ford. The Ash has a more pronounced grain pattern. Both cars used Mahogany veneer inner panels.

Photos from Yahoo.com images

1948 Custom Ford Sportsman

When your heart is set on having a Ford Sportsman, but there's none to be had, and if there was you might not be able to afford it, you do the next best thing you build one. That's just what an enterprising owner of this 1948 Ford convertible did. Staying as close to the look of a real Sportsman as possible (probably after studying photos) without actually building an entirely new body. Most wood was applied atop metal.

Photos from carrosysclassico.com

105

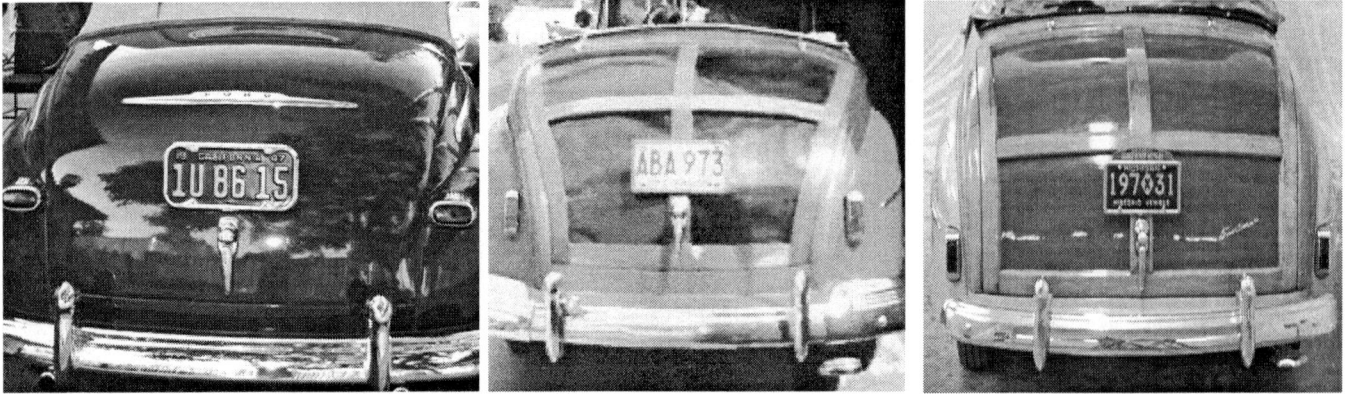

I believe the only fabrication done was to build a new deck lid. The Original steel deck lid was too bulbous, the deck lid needed to be somewhat flat. As seen in the photos.

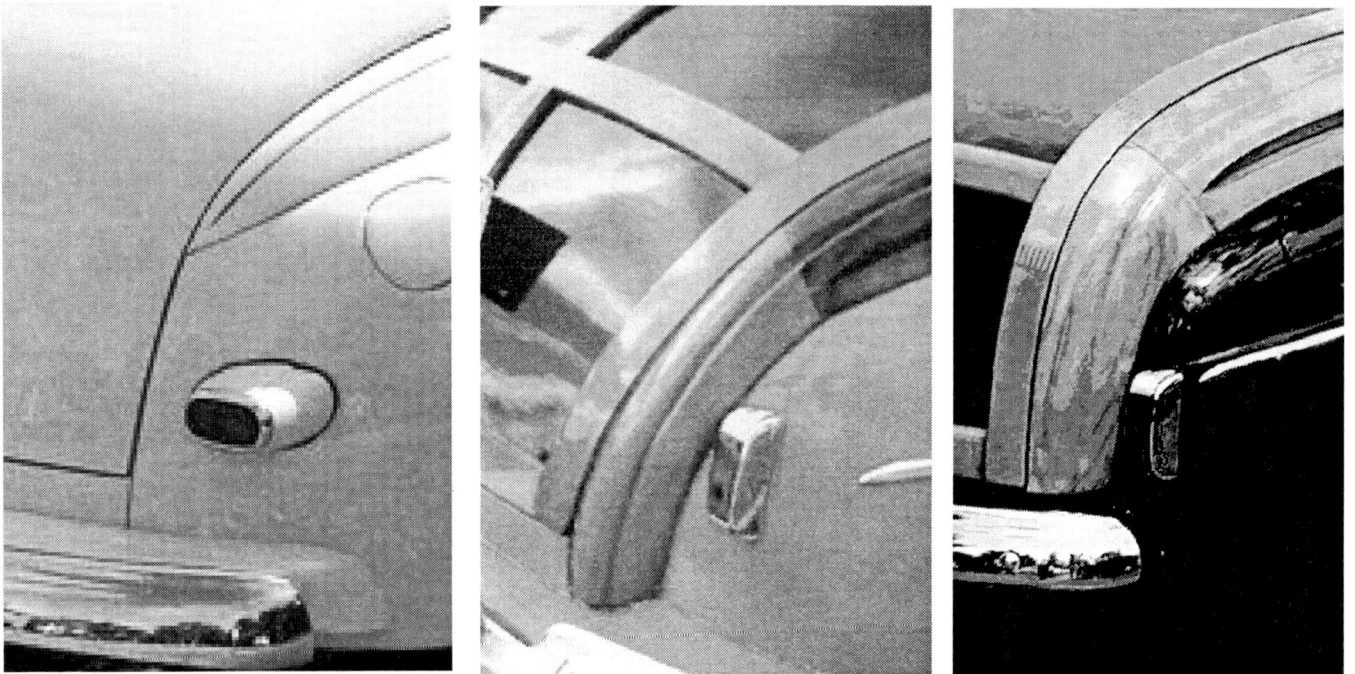

Following the belt line down to the splash pan necessitated trimming the rear fender.

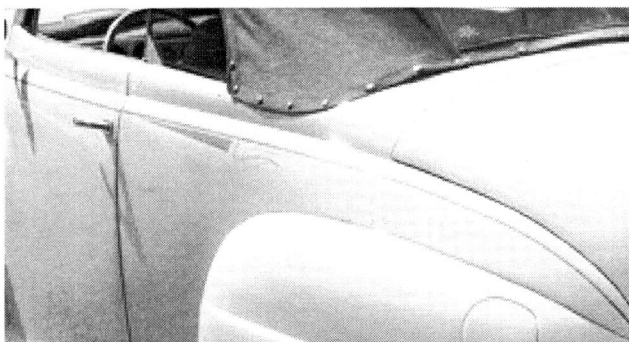

Besides the deck lid, one of the biggest challenges was following the steel belt-line.

Photos from carrosysclaasico.com

1940 Ford Custom Woodie Convertible

Woodies seem to come in all flavors. This one based on the 1940 Ford Convertible is more a piece of art. On close examination you can see that the wood is sculpted. It appears that the body is structurally wood. Built more like a station wagon.

Photos from Yahoo.com images

It's all in the details and this car has a lot of detail to look at, evidence that skilled hands were at work in building the "Woodie". Check out the sculpted tail lights, the deck lid, recessed license tag and the exhaust ports. You will also note that the leading edge door post follows the "A" pillar up the windshield frame. Interesting!

Photos from Yahoo.com images

Slightly Modified

Mike DeViriendt appreciates vintage cars, but he also appreciates performance, so his 1946 Ford Sportsman is: "slightly modified".

The body, number 104, built in July 1946, was left pretty much stock. The wood was left unmolested and the only modification to the sheet metal was lengthening of the bumper splash pans. The license plate was moved from the deck lid to the rear bumper and a modified 1940 Ford license frame was used to house the plate. The interior was left stock and upholstered in red leather with tan carpets.

The original engine block was rebuilt to 276 cubic inches, 12 volt system, using a 4 inch Mercury crankshaft, Ardun OHV heads, Austin Manifold, three 2 barrel Stromberg carbs and a Walker radiator. Coupled to the rebuilt original 3 speed transmission. A Columbia rear with overdrive was added. The axels were dropped to give it a low slung Street Rod look. The front wheels are 15x6 with 640x15 tires and rear wheels are 15x8 with 740x15 tires.

All the work was first class, insuring a high quality 1946 Ford Sportsman, *"slightly modified"*.

Photos from Mike DeViriendt

The "A" pattern wood body is unmolested, the only change is in moving the license plate from the deck lid to the rear bumper. Actually this was an improvement.

Above, The interior was left pretty much stock and re-done in Red leather. Seat belts were added. Floor covering is Tan carpeting. **Left,** The original engine block was re-worked and increased to 276 cubic inches. Ardun OHV heads and Stromberg carbs were installed.

Photos from Mike DeViriendt

110

El nuevo Ford Convertible 1946 para Deportistas

¡Por dentro y por fuera . . . jamás se ha visto un automóvil semejante! Los diseñadores Ford han combinado la elegancia del automóvil cerrado con la conveniencia del "toque de un botón" del convertible.

Sólo toque un botón . . . y en 30 segundos pueden levantarse o bajarse simultánea o individualmente la capota y las cuatro ventanas. ¡Tiene Ud., a su elección, un automóvil abierto o cerrado en sólo medio minuto!

Acomoda un baúl. Hay sitio de sobra en el nuevo compartimiento de equipaje . . . lo mismo que en los anchos asientos de cuero con suficiente espacio para acomodar a seis personas mayores.

¡HAY UN *Ford* EN SU FUTURO!

Diamond in the Rough

In his youth Richard Adams Sr, worked as a mechanic at a Ford garage in MeHenry, Illinois. Where a local resident had her 1946 Ford Sportsman serviced on a regular basis. It was love at first sight. He was drawn to the gleaming wood body and vowed that one day he would own such a car.

Over the next five decades the desire for owning a Sportsman never left him. In 1993 he launched a search for his dream car. The search was not easy. The car was scarce, but he was not deterred. Finally in 1997 the right opportunity came along, he had found his dream car, it was perfect !

Richard's 1947 Sportsman had been completely restored by Terry Howash of Classic Car Craft, in Ontario, Canada. The original car was a junk yard cast off, a derelict, brought back to life. Patience, tenacity and craftsmanship went into the restoration. The car was completely disassembled, the crushed windshield frame and dash were replaced with parts from a donor car. What was left of the wood was removed and a new body was fabricated to factory specs, using Canadian Maple, Birdseye Maple and Fiddleback Maple, the finished body would be very difficult, if not impossible to duplicate. NOS parts were used wherever possible. The car has a Columbia rear end with overdrive. Accessories include a radio, heater, side view mirrors, white wall tires and fog lights.

Once the car was home, Richard began attacking the details. He was determined to make it even better. Not satisfied with some of the fit, he dissembled the doors, reworked the window hydraulics and refitted the doors. He made sure every nut, bolt and clip were correct and everything on the car worked properly. When he was finished the car looked and worked like the day it came off the line; spanking new. Maybe even better.

Satisfied with his detailing, the Pheasant Red, paint code 14230, 1947 Ford Sportsman with the "C" pattern wood body was taken to the Early Ford V-8 Grand National in Dearborn, Michigan; where it received the coveted *"Dearborn Award"*, first time out.

Richard enjoys his Sportsman and drives it regularly to car shows and cruise-ins and say's, *"I love to drive it on Sundays. It's a great car and the wooden body really attracts attention. I guess I've got a mixture of sawdust and oil in my veins."*

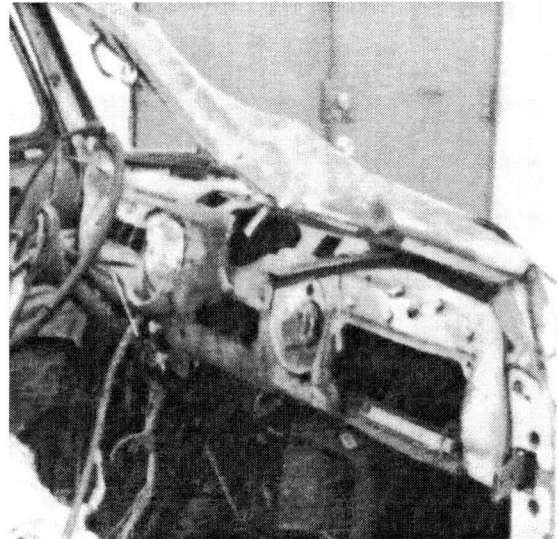

Twenty years ago a derelict such as this Sportsman would have been relegated to the scrap heap without giving it a second thought. It would have been folly to try and restore. Today nothing is impossible. Given the time and resources, there are enough craftsman around to take on most any challenge. Eying the photos may look doubtful.

Photos courtesy V-8 Times/Richard Adams Sr.

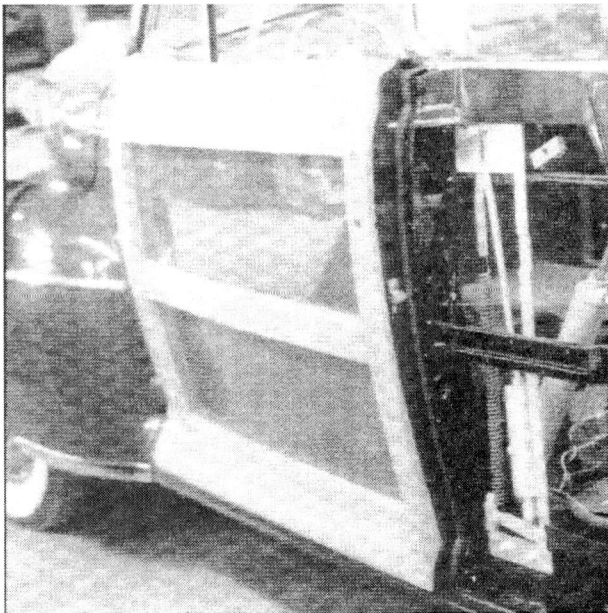

The dashboard and windshield frame were replaced with parts from a donor car. In addition a complete new wood body was fabricated. The frame was refurbished and all the mechanic 's were rebuilt, using NOS parts wherever possible.

Photos courtesy V-8 Times/Richard Adams Sr.

What once was scrap is now a work of art, a "Diamond". Its hard to imagine that this award winning example (it won the coveted *Dearborn Award* at the Early V-8 Club Grand National in Dearborn, Michigan) was once a total wreck, a junk yard cast-off.

Photos courtesy V-8 Times/Richard Adams Sr.

LIMITED EDITION
1948 FORD SPORTSMAN

*Shown approximately actual size
(Scale 1:24; 3" in width
8 1/2" in length)*

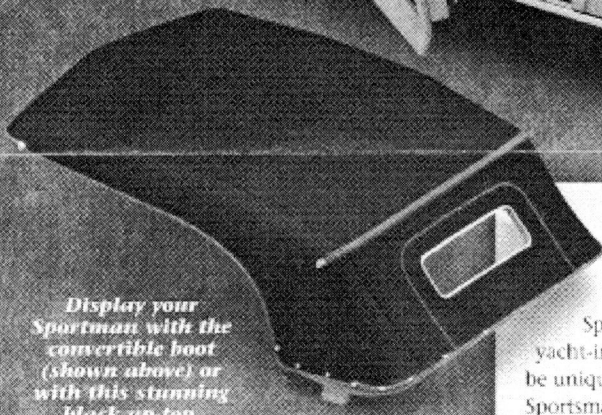

*Display your
Sportsman with the
convertible boot
(shown above) or
with this stunning
black up-top.
Your choice!*

When automobile production geared up again after World War II, the Ford Motor Company needed an all-out "halo car" to draw customers into its showrooms. The Sportsman was that car. The Dearborn designers took Ford's top-of-the-line Special DeLuxe and raised the bar, creating a drop-dead gorgeous, yacht-inspired hardwood trimmed body for an automobile that would be unique in the low-priced field. Like most ultra-exclusive models, the Sportsman was a limited production number, and those that did sell were highly coveted then — and now!

In 1948, only 28 Sportsman convertibles left the plant. Few of those survive today, making this vintage the rarest of all Sportsmen! Now, the Danbury Mint brings you an incredibly masterful 1:24 scale die-cast

*Shown approximately actual size
(Scale 1:24; 3" in width)*

**Limited Edition!
Produced for 6
months only!**

1948

1948

Miscellaneous

Can't find a Sportsman? Can't afford a Sportsman? All is not lost. How about a scale model. There are several out there, from N Scale to 1:18. Something for every one. We've come across a N Scale in plastic. A 1:47 die-cast, a 1:33 die-cast, a very nice 1:25 from Danbury Mint and several 1:18. And if you can find one, a vintage balsa wood model. Check 'em out.

Plastic 1:33   Die-Cast 1:43 upper, 1:18 lower   Vintage Balsa Model

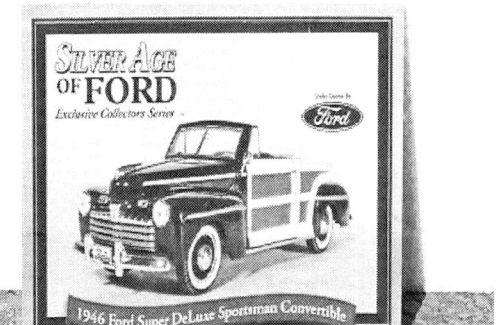

Die-Cast 1:18   Die-Cast 1:32

Photos from Dave Kuffel Collection and various sources

FORD'S OUT FRONT!

WITH THE NEW 1946 FORD SPORTSMAN

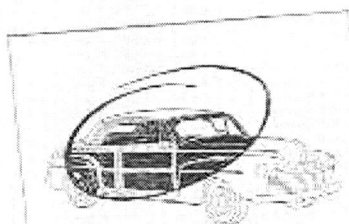

Big New 100 h.p. V-8

makes Ford the liveliest performer of all the low-priced cars! New 4-ring aluminum pistons make the big Ford V-8 thrifty on gas and oil! Its extra power is easily controlled by new over-sized hydraulic brakes.

This Bright New Beauty

combines station wagon smartness with the convenience of a convertible! Just touch a button . . . and the top and all four windows are raised or lowered automatically, in just seconds. Top up or top down, it's a beauty for looks . . . a new kind of car!

It Takes a Trunk

There's room galore in this new luggage compartment . . . just as there's room galore for six grownups in the wide, leather seats! Outside and inside, there never was a car like this before!

THERE'S A

Ford

IN YOUR FUTURE

Resources and References

Resources:

Robert Brown and Son dba "The Sportsman Restoration Shop"
Restoration and Body Builder-30 years experience
2860 Butler Creek Road
Sdero Woolley, Washington 98284
sportsmanwoodie@earthlink.net
www.rbwoodies.com

National Woodie Club
PO Box 6134
Lincoln, NE 68506-6134
Email: johnlee@neb.rr.com
www.nationalwoodieclub.com

Early Ford V-8 Club
PO Box 1715
Maple Grove, MN 55311
Email: info@earlyfordv8.org
www.earlyfordv8.org

References:

"Fabulous Ford Woodies" Lorin Sorenson
"Illustrated History of Ford" George Damman
"Great American Woodies and Wagons" Donald Narus
"Ford Postwar Flatheads" James H. Moloney
"Standard Catalog of Ford" John Gunnell
"Special Interest Autos- Mar/Apr 1996" Tim Howley
"Seventy-One Society Newsletters" Tom Garrett
"Early Ford V-8 Times"
"Hemmings Book of Mercurys"

This book is available as an E book in Full Color

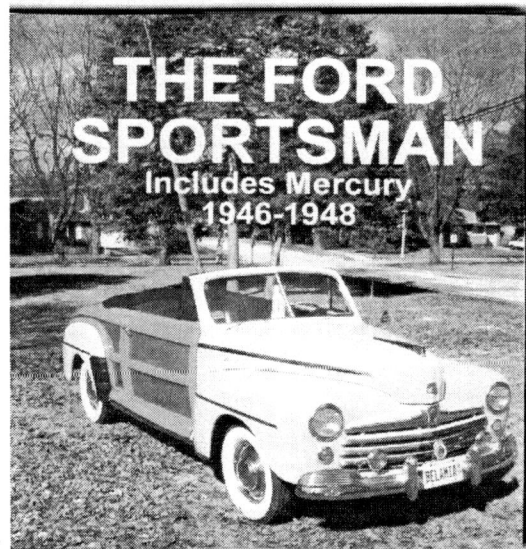

THE FORD SPORTSMAN
Includes Mercury
1946-1948

Order at:

www.newalbanybooks.com

About the Author

Don Narus has been writing about "Woodies" since 1973. His first book: "Chrysler's Wonderful Woodie" was the first time anyone had written about a single Woodie marque. He followed that with "Great American Woodies and Wagons" in 1977; which became the Woodie Bible. In 1988 a revised updated version of "Chrysler's Wonderful Woodie" was released, followed by a revised edition of "Great American Woodies and Wagons" in 1995. Since then two other Chrysler Woodie books were written and released in 2009 and 2010. In 2007 Don and his son Mark formed New Albany Books. Don was the founder of The Town & Country Owners Registry, and is currently a member of the National Woodie Club/ Town & Country Chapter and The Early Ford V8 Club. His Sportsman connection goes back to a barn find, when he uncovered and purchased a 1946 Mercury Sportsman in 1974.

Other Books Available on-line

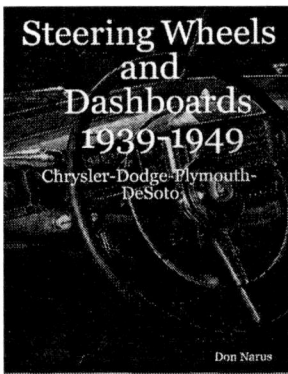

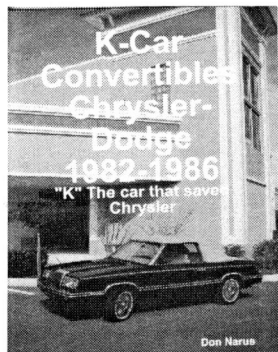

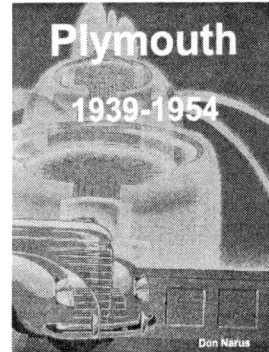

www.newalbanybooks.com